Planepack:

EXPLORING THE WORLD

Interviews by Slobodanka Graham

Published by BGPublishers
www.bgpublishers.com.au
© 2024 Bobby Graham Publishers
www.planepack.com.au

All rights reserved
Cover and book design by Elise Knotek, Stripe Design
with illustrations by Slobodanka Graham

Digital editions produced by SunTecIndia
www.suntecindia.com

First edition 2024

The interviews in this book first
appeared in Planepack 2017-18
www.planepack.com.au

ISBN 978-0-6451402-9-3

How to dress and pack like a royal rock star

Vicky Kidd-Gallichan is a Canberra couture gown, corset and costume designer. *Rockstars and Royalty* designs and produces amazing gowns. I chatted to her about her inspiration, about environmentally sustainable fashion—and travelling with voluptuous and unique clothes.

𝓟𝓟: **You've got an online clothing business called Rockstars and Royalty. It's a great name. Can you tell us a little bit more about the business?**

VKG: I've been a designer for nearly twenty years and during that time I've been designing one off couture gowns for my clients. That's where my name comes from, because I do very elaborate dresses, so the royalty part is my big tulle gowns, my big princess royalty gowns, and the rockstar part is my more … out there range. I've done a lot of black wedding dresses and red wedding dresses and really over-the-top stuff. I love embellishments and crystals.

I've reached the point where I've decided to take the brand online, and I'm bringing a little bit of the couture experience to online shopping. Within each design on the website, you can choose different elements, so you can choose different lengths and colours and fabrics and embellishments within each dress or skirt or corset, and the couture part is that you can mix and match sizing at the bust, waist, and hip.

From all my years making one-off gowns for clients, I know that there are so many women who do not fit into standard sizing, so this is a way to get a better fit for people who aren't a standard size. If you're a size fourteen bust and twelve waist, you can order a dress that's going to fit you.

My long-term goals are to grow the brand, to add more designs; my dream is to do away with sizing altogether. Everyone will order just their size—it doesn't matter what size you are, what height you are, what body type you are—and my dream is to link body scanning and patternmaking, so you'll be able to design a dress and order it exactly to all of your measurements. I don't believe in splitting things into 'plus size' or anything like that; I think everyone's fabulous and should be able to wear what they want to wear. My dream is for you to be able to go onto the Rockstars and Royalty website, design the dress of your dreams, and order it in your size.

_PP_: I love the mix of technology and design, but I also like the fairytale princess aspect of your clothes. What does that do for the buyer of your clothes?

VKG: It makes my customers feel fabulous. Working with couture clients for a long time, I've had a lot of girls come in who feel like they're not good enough to wear a dress. They feel like they're the wrong shape, because we're being fed these ridiculous standards by the fashion industry and the media all the time. They come in and say, 'Oh, I'm too big to wear that; I'm too short to do that.'

And then you make them this dress and they put it on: you see them and they stand up tall, and they just say, 'I feel amazing'. And that confidence lasts long after they've taken the dress off: they realise that they are beautiful. Everyone is beautiful. I believe everyone is fabulous, and should be able to wear what they want to wear.

Just putting someone in something that's made for them, that fits them properly in a shape and a colour that they love, that they've had input into ... it's a huge confidence-building moment for everyone, and I could see the change in their stance, in their eyes, and in their smile as well. And that's what makes it worth it for me.

PP: **You can see it in the photos of people wearing your wedding dresses: that confidence and sense of self comes through. You mentioned your background and how you grew out of a traditional business, but what was it that really inspired you to design this particular kind of fashion?**

VKG: It's my love of anything over the top. I've got a hot pink mohawk at the moment. I'm covered in tattoos. I learned to sew because I didn't want to wear what everyone else was wearing. I've always, right from when I was preteen—maybe eleven, twelve years old—wanted to wear what I wanted to wear. My mom taught me to sew so I could make things. I used to op-shop back then and upcycle things to make them my own. I know there's a lot of people who call their friends and say, 'What are you wearing?' so they make sure they all wear the same things. I ring my friends and say, 'What are you wearing?' so I can make sure I don't wear the same thing.

I'm not afraid to experiment, and my designs are very much a reflection of my style; I want to encourage other people to have the confidence to be themselves. A lot of the time people are dressing like everyone else, because they don't have the confidence to stand out, even though they'd really love to give it a go. I'm hoping to inspire people with the confidence to wear what they want to wear, not what they're being told to wear by trends, and by the big fast-fashion brands. I want people to find their own style, find themselves, and it's a big turning point in your confidence when you do find yourself.

When you find your size, you put on something that you really love, that makes you feel fabulous. You're like, 'I can take on the world today!'

PP: **When I met you recently at the Canberra Wise Women event, you had little bags on display. Can you tell us a little bit more about those?**

VKG: I've just launched a range of bags and purses. For me, the environmental impact of the fashion industry—the negative effect that a lot of fashion brands are having on the planet—is just heartbreaking. The fashion industry—depending on what source you find, it's either the second or the third biggest polluting industry in the world, after oil. Oil's the first. The waste we're producing … it is unsustainable to keep making fashion as we're making it, to keep buying fast fashion. We've gone into this cycle of buying something and only wearing it once because it's cheap, or it's out of trend, and then it ends up in the op shops, which are inundated with more clothes than they can deal with, or that they can sell.

I believe we need to really start shopping differently. I think some of the responsibility lies with the consumer and their purchasing choices; they've got to decide to buy things that are coming from a more ethical background. And some of the responsibility lies with the manufacturers. I'm already manufacturing on demand, so I don't have a lot of stock lying around waiting to be sold, hoping that someone wants the green in a size ten.

So the bags: a new collection I've launched to use up my scrap fabric. I've got bags of sequins and satin that sat around the studio, that I didn't want to throw away because I can't just put a bag in the bin and send it to landfill. The bags are my way to use up the scraps that are too small to use. The panels are scrap panels, and I'm making pretty little embellished bags.

I'm also making denim bags, using jeans that are too worn or too stained or damaged to be sold through an op shop, so I've incorporated denim into the collection.

𝒫𝒫: **I'm interested in your philosophy of reusing and repurposing materials and fabric and content in order to help us preserve the environment.**

𝒱𝒦𝒢: One of the important things, one of my important messages about shipping more sustainably and having a more sustainable wardrobe is to look at what you already own. So many times you go out and you buy something when you've got something similar already in your wardrobe at home. I encourage people to go back to their wardrobe, look at what they've got, and think about wearing things in different ways. This is where it really links in with your message of packing lightly.

I think we get into the habit of making a uniform of our clothes, so that we always wear 'that' top with 'that' skirt, or 'that' blouse with 'those' jeans. But we can mix and match those and have a whole new look. Especially when we're travelling, but in everyday life as well, we need to look at what we already own and think about different ways to put it together. We can take one belt and put it around a dress and make that dress look different, but we can [also] wear that belt with jeans or with trousers. It's really important to build a capsule wardrobe that you can mix and match and rewear.

My other key message is to buy just a few really good-quality pieces. Those pieces that you love, that are your style, that you will wear over and over again. They're going to be more expensive, but buy well and buy less. And if you know you're going to wear that beautiful coat for years to come, or that corset is going to go under or over everything, spend more money on it. By the time you've bought so much of this cheap, fast fashion, it soon adds up, and you might as well have bought one good piece.

That will help you in your packing: 'Oh, I can take this one blouse, but it will go with these jeans, this skirt … and I can add a scarf, I can add a jacket and rewear this blouse in five, six different ways while I'm away.'

PP: I know that you are going away. And are you travelling light?

VKG: I am going to see my family in France for Christmas, so I will be travelling light in terms of clothes, but not in terms of all the presents I'm taking with me. I think three-quarters of my case is filled with gifts that I'm taking over, but that means I am having to really think about the clothing that I'm taking. I'm heading from an Australian summer to a French winter, and we're stopping over in Hong Kong on the way back as well. I'm trying to pick outfits that I can layer for winter, and then wear unlayered the other way.

The gifts are making me think very carefully about what I can pack, and what I can carry on. I will be taking checked luggage, but beyond that, I'm having to really think about dresses I can put long-sleeved T-shirts under, that I can then wear without the T-shirts when we're in Hong Kong; dresses that I can put leggings or tights underneath and wear with boots while we're in France, and then I can take a pair of ballet flats and wear no tights under it for Hong Kong as well.

I've been op shopping for a couple of nice big cardigans to take. I've got a couple of nice chunky knits to put over things as well. Again, that layering.

PP: If you were to travel with one of your own skirts or dresses, which are quite ornate, how would you pack that?

VKC: I've made a lot of dresses over the years for clients who got married overseas, so they have had to pack wedding dresses. I make sure my clients tell me this upfront when we start the design process. We choose fabrics that aren't going to crumple, so no silk organza that's going to come out looking like screwed up tissue paper at the other end. We take that into account during the design process.

Some airlines are really helpful, and will let you hang a gown [in a] cover on the plane. Some are not so helpful.

PP: Is a gown cover like a suit bag?

VKC: Like a suit bag, yes, but a bit bigger, normally. I do try to encourage people to take it in their hand luggage. You don't need the stress of worrying about whether it's going to come out at the other end when you arrive at your destination. It's amazing some of the things we've managed to get into one piece of hand luggage. I've got a client who just got married in Las Vegas, and we managed to fit—she had a huge hooped dress—and we managed to get the hoop, the skirt, the overskirt and the corset all into hand luggage. It arrived there and she got married, and they actually went travelling around America for a few weeks for their honeymoon, so she posted it back and she managed to get it squeezed into a little box to post it back.

I've done a lot of dresses for girls who have taken them all over the world for weddings, and it's definitely something ... with my online collection. The sequin fabric is heavy, but it does pack up really well, because it doesn't crease. At the other end, the sequin dresses are really good to transport.

PP: **What do you take in your carry-on bag, or things that you actually take with you on the plane?**

VKG: I take my electronics. I always take my camera and my laptop with me, because I don't like to put them in the hold, just because I worry about losing them. Plus I can't sleep on planes, so I take my laptop so I can work on something. For this trip, I've been filming YouTube videos, and then I'm going to do some editing on the plane.

I'll have my laptop, my headphones, my camera and my Kindle so I can read as well. A bit of make-up, some skin products, toothbrush, toothpaste. Just the basic hygiene things to keep me refreshed over a flight.

When we leave here, we're on the coach at five am from Canberra, then we fly out from Sydney at midday. We'll get to France at 5:30 am on Christmas Eve. Then we have to pick up a car and drive. So it's a really long journey.

I take snacks as well. This is the first time I've travelled since I've been vegan, so I'm a little dubious about what food I might get on the aeroplane.

PP: **I don't think that you're going to get much that you're going to be able to eat. Will you have to take your own supply?**

VKG: I will be packing a lot of snacks to keep me going for this whole journey.

PP: **What sorts of snacks will you take with you?**

VKG: Lots of nuts and nut bars, and fruit. Going out of Australia, that's okay. Coming back in, it's not. But leaving is fine.

PP: **You'll have eaten it all on the way there, and you'll have to bring in something French on the way back.**

VKG: Yes, definitely. And we're stopping in—I think we have five hours in Shanghai airport. Might be able to get something nice on the way over as well. We'll have a little break there. I think it's nice to have that sort of break to really give you a chance to get up and walk around and refresh and have some food and feel relaxed before getting on the next flight.

I've been on a flight going to Europe before, when we've had an hour, hour-and-a-half layover, and it's just manic. There's the worry that if you're late, you're going to miss your next flight.

This way takes the stress out of it. I think five hours is a good time: it's not too long, not too short.

𝓟𝓟: What for you has been the most challenging aspect of running your own business?

𝓥𝓚𝓖: Trying to do everything myself. I'm a single person doing everything at the moment, and so time management is really important; I'm really careful with how I spend my time and how I divide up my time to make sure I get the most out of it, but I still work long hours. It can be very tiring. I know I'm reaching the end of the year now; it's got to the end today, 15 December, I am exhausted. I've reached that point where I'm really ready for a break.

Managing my time and being responsible for everything, I find that really hard at times. I sometimes wish I had a business partner to bounce ideas off, or just to take some of the responsibility. But at the same time, I love doing everything, because it gives me control.

I know that when I'm working, I'm working for something for myself. It makes it a lot easier when you're there till midnight, for the fourth night in a row, sewing.

𝓟𝓟: What advice do you have for women who are keen to enter the fashion business?

𝓥𝓚𝓖: You need to be passionate. It needs to be something that is in your blood, that is your life force, because it's a horribly hard industry. It needs to be something that you are really passionate about. You need to be strong, you need to fight for what you want. And enter it with morals. It's hard to keep those morals intact, because when you need to make money, sometimes you think, 'Oh, maybe it would be easier just to buy some cheap stuff from China and sell it and make some money.' But keep your morals and your ethics intact as you do it, and it will be better in the long run.

PP: **It's been lovely talking to you. I'm looking forward to going to your studio now to have a look at some of your clothes.**

VKG: Fantastic, thank you.

PP: **Thank you very much for your time, bon voyage. I hope you enjoy France.**

VKG: Merci.

ROCKSTARS AND ROYALTY

rockstarsroyalty.com

How to win space with your Airpocket travel bag

Whenever I travel long haul, I like to stretch my legs. I'm not always able to do that if my handbag is jammed under the seat in front of me. These days I'm using Airpocket to transform my flying experience from discomfort to cushy comfort. I chatted to Trish Smith and Tanya Corcoran, the owners of Airpocket.

PP: **What is Airpocket?**

AP: Airpocket is a slim compact bag that you can take on the plane with you and it's for organising all of the essentials that you like to have with you at your seat. It's designed so that you can pop in your glasses, your iPod, iPad, reading glasses and lots of things; when you arrive on the plane you just slot it straight into the seat-back pocket of the aeroplane. Everything is fixed during the flight, then when you leave the plane you take it with you and nothing gets left behind. It's made from neoprene and it contains pockets and dividers to keep everything organised and protected. Neoprene is a soft and malleable material that molds and shapes around pretty much whatever you put in inside, and it protects things from being scratched.

PP: **What prompted you to design Airpocket?**

AP: I was on a flight home from Brisbane and we were all boarding. I had sat down and there was a queue forming in the aisle and I looked up to see a young lady blocking the aisle while she ruffled around in her handbag looking for all of the things that she wanted. She stood in the aisle, and she had a make-up bag and the magazine and what have you. I just sort of watched her doing this, thinking that was a bit inconvenient for her and everybody waiting in the aisle and it would have been quicker had she been able to take all of those things out in one go and sit down comfortably; that was the concept and the idea sort of quickly formed from there. I was just inspired, I think I sort of drew a rough diagram of it on the back of a boarding pass ... and that was how it got started.

PP: **You funded Airpocket with Kickstarter. How was that experience?**

AP: The wonderful thing about Kickstarter is that it is a great way to test your idea in the market without too much money upfront. You don't make it first and then try to sell it. You test the idea first, see whether people are interested to buy it, see whether they think it's a good idea and if they do, you also raise the money to get going. It became apparent fairly early on in the piece that I wasn't going to be able to launch this idea without some sort of financial help externally. So being able to test the idea was really an attractive proposition. That's how we decided to move that way.

PP: **You have two other products. Can you tell us about those?**

AP: As part of the Kickstarter campaign, you have a target and what people typically do is add what are called 'stretch goals', so if you meet certain financial targets you can add another product to that and your backers will select to purchase as well. Trish designed the Travel Book, which is a travel wallet. We call it a Travel Book, but it's function is as a travel wallet.

It can hold up to eight passports, and I think Trish was inspired to design something like this because she has a friend who has dual citizenship, as do her children and husband. When they travel they can carry up to eight passports.

I think there's a gap in the market for something that can hold all those passports and we all know that mum is usually the one who carries everybody's belongings.

The Travel Book was predominantly designed for families or multiple passports; however, I only have one passport and I use it to travel with. It can also hold all your travel documents, credit cards or—you know— regular flying program cards, business cards, etc. And it can hold up to a B5 notepad, so some people actually even use it at meetings as a nice little folder.

The third product is the Amenities Case. The Amenities Case has a clear top and it's designed for loose items like chargers; I use mine for [things like] lip gloss and hand cream, particularly for long haul flights. I like to be able to get up during the flight and brush my teeth and put some eye cream on and have a little bit of a freshen up, so I put all of those bits and pieces in my Amenities Case, which is designed to fit into one of the pockets in the Airpocket. So when I get on the flight I have got my Amenities Case, I have got my phone, my headphone, my pen—the best thing ever so when you are filling out the forms [for Customs].

I always leave my pen up in the overhead locker and have to get up after I have settled. The first time I used my Airpocket and they gave me the arrival documentation, I was so excited that all I had to do was reach for my pen!

For me the Airpocket, the Travel Book, the Amenities Case is all about convenience.

I like to be organised. I travel light and that extra level of organisation has really enhanced the whole travel experience.

PP: Are you both light travellers?

AP: We have different approaches, which is interesting because we look at our products from different points of view in that respect. We both very much like to be organised. I probably travel quite a bit—ten to fifteen trips a year, domestic and international—and I tend to just travel with one of the hard-shell light carry-on bags. I can comfortably fit everything I need in there, for anywhere from a long weekend to a two-week trip. I am a roller. I roll things. I find I can get more in. I use packing cells as well. It keeps things together. I always travel with a laundry bags so I can separate grubby things from everything else and the biggest challenge is reducing how many pairs of shoes that I take.

𝓟𝓟: How many pairs of shoes do you take?

𝓐𝓟: Well I try to wear bulky shoes on flights so they don't take up space in my case. Depending if I'm traveling somewhere warm I try to take a pair of shoes that I can be worn casually but also dress up so that they are multifunctional. I try to get away with two [pairs], I can only get one more pair in, but always I have to take slippers. I am not prepared to run the risk that the hotel won't have slippers. So I always take slippers with me.

𝓟𝓟: What about you, Trish?

𝓐𝓟: Well, I have had some disastrous overseas holidays. I can remember going on my very first big overseas trip. I went to the US for three months after I graduated from university and I took a bag that was so heavy and so big I couldn't lift it. And looking back I had no strategy at all for packing other than 'take everything'. So fortunately I have come a long way from those dark days, but I am still quite inspired by Tanya's . . .

𝓟𝓟: Minimalist approach?

𝓐𝓟: Very much so; in fact, when we weigh the bags at the airport. I have always got my eyes on the numbers. Dammit, she's always a few kilos lighter than me!

But I am learning. I did a trip a few years ago where I travelled from Australia into Bangkok where it was very hot and then I spent a couple of weeks in Norway where it was a bit cooler and I was determined to take just carry on. I managed it, so I learnt that less is more, I think. I tend to fill the space available, so I have recently bought a smaller suitcase to force myself to get a bit more strategic, but packing cells and rolling is definitely the way to go.

PP: **How much does Airpocket weigh?**

AP: Empty, it weighs 385 grams. So it's quite light. We spent a lot of time thinking about what material we'd make it out of, obviously the lighter the better for travelling. The great thing about neoprene is that it is quite light, but it also provides that cushioning so we don't need an extra layer of padding in it; the padding is part of it.

PP: **Will it protect my iPad, my phone, my glasses?**

AP: I wear glasses and when I want to go to sleep I can take them off and I don't even need to put them back inside their case. Neoprene doesn't have anything on it to scratch; there is nothing inside the Airpocket that will scratch anything.

I would add to that: one of the reasons for neoprene is it's quite robust. We wanted to balance weight for convenience, but also use a fabric that's robust, that can bear the rigours of travel.

𝓟𝓟: Inevitably something is spilt on your bag or on yourself. Is it is easy to clean Airpocket?

𝓐𝓟: Yes it is, and that's another thing, you are probably familiar with wetsuits from Australia and the surfing culture. That was another reason why we selected the neoprene. You can just wipe it off and it's good to go; it doesn't retain the moisture, so it's great from that point of view.

𝓟𝓟: Should I carry on a handbag as well?

𝓐𝓟: The Airpocket wasn't designed to replace your handbag. It was designed to handle a level of convenience whilst traveling. I don't carry a handbag when I travel; I tend to leave my handbag and I just carry my phone and credit cards and cash. I travel with a tote because I have other bulkier items that I might tak; a larger laptop device, my scarf. I put those in my tote and that tote is my carry-on bag, and then when I get on the plane I take the Airpocket out of my tote and put the tote and everything I don't need during the flight in the overhead bin.

𝓟𝓟: I like that you produced the Airpocket with a long strap. What was your thinking around that?

𝓐𝓟: That was a change we made to the design during the Kickstarter campaign. We had a lot of our backers ask if we were going to be providing it with a shoulder strap, and that comes back to how I thought the Airpocket would be used by people. I didn't think that anyone would want to use it as a separate standalone bag.

I thought you'd slip it over the extended handle of your suitcase or carry it under your arm and then pop it into something bigger than that. So people said, 'We like to wear it as a bag.' We asked our backers after the campaign, because we keep touch with them through the Kickstarter platform, 'How many of you would like us to provide a strap?' and many people said yes. So we went back to the manufacturer and said, 'We're going to need to create that,' as previously we just had a small wrist strap. It's been really successful as a crossbody bag where you can shorten the strap so that it's more like a handbag.

PP: **You mentioned that you can slip Airpocket over the handles of your luggage bag as well?**

AP: It has a wide band across the back that's a luggage trolley sleeve, because when you are running through the airport you don't want your bags banging against your shoulder and it's perfectly safe to slip over a handle. And then it's sitting really quite neatly on top of your suitcase so if you are standing in a queue at check in or through immigration, it's easy to reach in and get what you need.

𝓟𝓟: **What future plans are there for Airpocket?**

𝓐𝓟: We have just come back from our second visit to the Las Vegas Travel Goods Association trade show. It's been really great to meet in America, with American retailers and buyers and start to think how we can expand, because at the moment we sell online all over the world and we are looking at our options—you know, retail outlets. So going to an international trade show gives us access to the sorts of opportunities that might be a bit harder to reach from Canberra.

We have a couple of new products in the pipeline that continue the 'organisation' theme. We would like to expand our range to look at other products that will enhance your life, whether that will be day-to-day or when travelling. I think generally most will have a travel theme, given that that's one of the things that we like to do. So we are currently working on some designs that we hope to be releasing later in the year or the first quarter of next year.

AIRPOCKET

airpocket.com.au

How to catch an emperor penguin and what to wear in the Antarctic

Adventure, danger, exploration and excitement: who hasn't at some stage wanted a thrilling lifestyle? I chatted to Kieran Lawton, Antarctic explorer, who's experienced what the rest of us only dream about.

𝒫𝒫: **Shackleton, Scott and Ross are famous Antarctic explorers, bringing to mind daring, bravery and the romance of polar expeditions. For some time you were an Antarctic explorer. Can you tell me, is it really like that?**

𝒦ℒ: Wow. Well, I guess those guys are from a certain era where they really were exploring new ground. And, well, to be honest that's still possible. I've done a lot of work in the Antarctic and the Antarctic is a big place. Think of a place one-and-a-half times the size of Australia, that gets 30,000 visitors a year and they're nearly all tourists and they all go to one area, generally. So there's a lot of ground to explore. There is a lot of opportunity for daring, yes.

𝒫𝒫: **At different times you were an expedition leader, a mountain guide, a field training officer, and a biologist. Which of these was the most challenging for you? Can you talk to us a little bit about them?**

𝒦ℒ: I started working in polar regions as a biologist. One of my earlier experiences was over winter working on emperor penguins. They're the only animal species that's in the Antarctic in winter. They breed on the sea ice in the middle of winter and the male broods the egg while the female goes to sea, which can be hundreds of kilometres away across the sea ice. It's minus 30 every day and dark and windy and all that kind of thing.

Being a biologist down there is very interesting, but they are very long term gigs. At that time we were out on the ice for seven months, living in a shipping container. Life's kind of slow and you work away at it, whereas the other jobs—being an expedition leader or some of the more logistical jobs that I've done down there—are full of excitement and movement. They happen in summer; lots of people around, lots of activity. So quite different.

PP: When you went to Antarctica how did you get there?

KL: I've been doing it for 20 years. And most of my trips have been by boat, by ship, or by yacht. If you come to and from Australia, you're at least a week at sea, longer. Generally ten days.

The shortest route is from South America across the Drake Passage: you can do that in three days. If you're on a ship, a week. If you're on a yacht, longer … that's part of the adventure, I suppose.

I have flown in in more recent years. There's an airstrip on the Antarctic peninsula, the Australians have got an airstrip on this side now and there's one at McMurdo, south of New Zealand. So people do fly in a bit now. That's a different sort of experience because when you sail you get there gradually and it's a real journey. The wildlife emerges and coldness happens over a period of time. You kind of get immersed in it.

When you fly in it's a bit more like you go and look there. I'm a bit of a fan of sailing.

𝓟𝓟: **Where did you stay?**

𝓚𝓛: I had a variety of trips. Most people will stay on a vessel. People—95 per cent of them when they go as tourists or even as a scientist will go on a ship and stay on the ship—will not stay ashore. But a lot of the Antarctic coastline is either surrounded by sea ice or, in the case of the Antarctic peninsula which is south of South America, there are massive fjords so there's a lot of calm water and you can get right up close to the land. So you feel like you're a part of it. Obviously I've camped out a lot and stayed in field huts and static stations as well, so there's a whole variety. But I think most people will be staying on a boat close to shore in calm waters.

𝓟𝓟: **What's a typical day living in Antarctica?**

𝓚𝓛: When we were working on penguins or albatrosses I did a lot of work about understanding how those animals use their environment, what they feed on, where they go to feed, and how humans use those resources as well. Some of those species are in decline. Albatrosses, for example, get caught behind fishing boats. When I was working on emperor penguins there was a Russian krill fishery, but the albatrosses feed a lot on krill, so looking at those impacts I was trying to understand how those animals use their environment. We do that by tracking the animals. I worked at a time when satellite tracking was just being developed and we had basic devices called Time Depth Recorders for animals that lived at sea. If you pulled out an animal and glued the stuff on its back you could figure out where it was going, what it was feeding on, how deep it was diving, how it was using its environment.

We basically camped out with the species we were studying. We'd catch an emperor penguin, put on the device, let it go to sea to do its foraging trip and, when it comes back, get the data and see what it has been doing.

There'd be lots of camping out, getting up in the morning, finding an animal. Deploying a device, letting it go, and then perhaps waiting for several hours for animals coming in from the sea to see if one of your animals was there. And then catching that animal, taking the device back off.

Lots of time outside all day.

PP: How long was the day? Was there a lot of sunshine?

KL: Depends on the season. In winter obviously we're just working at night by headlamp. Well, working by day, but it's dark. And we would still work a normal day; nine hours, thereabouts. And in summer of course it's 24 hours of sunlight. So you tend to be more active and working longer. Long days.

PP: How do you catch a penguin?

KL: If it's a small penguin they're kind of easy. You can just go up and grab them with your hands. But emperors are big. They can be 25 to 30 kilograms and they're very mobile, because of the sea ice. They travel hundreds of kilometres across the sea ice, so they're good at it. Better than we are! We had quite an elaborate technique: we had a very long shepherd's crook. We would identify the penguin we wanted to catch and run after it. Instead of walking, it would flop onto its belly and toboggan. So it would be on its belly and push with its feet, which is really fast—it's about as fast as you can run. When it started doing that we'd run behind it and put this 12 foot (4 metre) long shepherd's crook around its shoulders and just pull it up. Then move up on to it and sort of hold it down; get it on its back. It's a bit of a technique.

PP: What did you like to photograph?

KL: There's so much to photograph there: wildlife and ice and the light on the ice and the ocean. All those things that change from hour to hour. The light is beautiful as well. So landscapes, really. Wildlife and landscapes.

𝒫𝒫: **What have you done with those photographs?**

𝒦ℒ: I used to be really keen and I got a lot published in calendars and magazines and that kind of thing. And I used to write stories. I worked on some shoots for film companies as well ... a bit of everything.

𝒫𝒫: **What did you pack when you'd travel to the Antarctic?**

𝒦ℒ: I'm thinking about the trip and what I'll need. To go to a cold place, I don't think you need a lot of clothes; you need just the right amount of clothes. That's one thing I try to do because space and weight is always at a premium. I do some research about where I'm going and what the sort of minimum temperatures are going to be. And how wet it's going to be—or dry—because the Antarctic is a big place. Some of it is maritime and quite warm so even in summer, say on the Antarctic peninsula, it will be wet-ish and kind of hovering around zero to minus two degrees. So you need certain clothes for that, which is quite different if you're going on land and it might be minus 20. It's quite dry. So you don't need waterproofs at all. But you need, you know, an extra layer of down or something like that. What I would do is research where I was going. Make sure I understood what the climate was like specifically and pack one set of clothes to cope with the coldest temperatures. And that would not be one big jacket or anything. That would be layers, then you're really adaptable.

𝓟𝓟: Can you describe what those clothes are?

𝓚𝓛: I would layer up. If I was going to the Antarctic peninsula and expected a minimum temperature of minus ten degrees in a maritime climate, I would have a wool thermal layer against the skin. And then a couple of layers of polyfleece pile over that. And then a down layer. And then a waterproof, windproof layer over that. So that means I can be comfortable at the coldest temperatures. I also have all the clothes I need for when it gets warmer as well. So you can just peel off some. I wouldn't be taking a big heavy jacket that filled up my suitcase. I would just be taking those layers, and not many duplicates. You know, even if you're going away for a while you always end up wearing the same clothes, right? So the only duplicates you need are underclothes and a spare pair of gloves and socks in case something goes wrong and you get wet. You don't actually need that much.

𝓟𝓟: What about footwear?

𝓚𝓛: I think you can get away with one pair of shoes if you select wisely and if you're trying to pack light. Footwear is massive and heavy. I would be taking a pair of hiking boots so I can walk on snow and ice and put a light set of crampons on. But also that I can wear in the plane and get around the ship and that kind of thing.

PP: If you were going on a short expedition how would you carry your gear with you?

KL: I guess it depends on the trip; you need to know that before you go. Plenty of times though it's been in a rucksack on your back. You might be on skis and you have your stuff in your rucksack.

So that's the way I always pack, just a rucksack, a minimum amount of clothes, and room to add those things like food or whatever I need. Everything that you could travel with you have to carry on your back. You need to be able to truckstop in boats and dinghies and carry it on rough surfaces. I've never been a wheels person.

PP: If someone were thinking of making a career for themselves in the Antarctic, how would they go about doing that?

KL: There are a number of ways to get into that field of work. Obviously there's the way I did it, which I think is the classic way, it's the way people's minds go: there are lots of scientists that work in the Antarctic. So you could embark on a scientific career. But there are also a lot of other avenues. And one of the ones is that there are more people doing trades than there are scientists—by about five to one—diesel mechanic, carpenter, electrician, plumber; all those people who are there to keep things working and keep stuff happening. People who deliver an essential service.

𝓟𝓟: Do you ever go back to the Antarctic?

𝓚𝓛: I am potentially going back in February of this year. I just pick and choose the trips now. My role now has become a bit of a local-knowledge person. So people get me into running trips when I know an area really well and they need someone who knows the area to make the trip amazing. I love going down there, but over twenty years, I've spent seven-and-a-half years in the Antarctic; I needed to do something else.

𝓟𝓟: Can you describe a highlight of your time in the Antarctic?

𝓚𝓛: It's very varied. And I spent such a long time there. The highlight of those places really is that they're beautiful places to be. And the rhythm of life is dictated by nature and the environment, and that is really lovely. But I think you're always there with people. And the relationships that you develop with people are much stronger, for me anyway. They seem to evolve much more quickly and be much stronger and quite long lasting. When you're in that kind of environment, when you're together all the time. So I guess the friendships are the things that are really meaningful to me.

PP: **Well it's been amazing talking to you, Kieran. Thank you very much for your insight into the Antarctic.**

KL: Thanks, Bobby. It's been a pleasure.

How packing cubes help you and your children travel light

CIare Idriss is an engineer, writer, mother and packer. She tells us about packing cubes—or, as she calls them, 'sophisticated pencil cases'—what they are; how she uses them, and how to colour code clothes when packing and travelling. It's all about compartmentalising your wardrobe.

_PP_: You are an engineer and you also run Practical Editing. Can you tell us about those?

_CJ_: As an engineer there are certain ways you might look at things, and that can be very logical and complex, and sometimes linear. A lot of people need that sort of approach to their writing and at the same time a lot of engineers don't like writing at all; they just want to do the work and then have the report magically appear.

The service I provide is helping people learn how to write better and frame and present their writing and get through it … and also to do the writing for them. They can give me the information and I can pump out the report.

_PP_: It's a great skill and a fabulous service that you offer, but I'm here to talk to you about travelling. Where was your last trip?

_CJ_: My last trip was to Cambodia. I went with Engineers Without Borders as a mentor.

_PP_: What does that mean?

_CJ_: Engineers Without Borders is an organisation in Australia. There are a few around the world. Some of them are connected to each other and others are not connected. The Engineers Without Borders in Australia work in a few areas promoting the idea of engineering in education. In Australia that's in universities, high schools, and primary schools. They also do projects where they support organisations overseas and in Australia to get what they need out of engineering: the technical ideas and technical advice while they're running the project.

There might be an organisation in Cambodia that needs some technical advice with the rainwater collection program that they're running and they'll partner with Engineers Without Borders and someone would come over and help there. For this, they can access our pool of knowledge.

PP: **What was your role in that trip?**

CJ: I was a mentor for university students who were there on an education program. They're learning about engineering in one of the communities or multiple communities. We went and visited and stayed in the community. The students come up with ideas that might be of use and present them to the community. If they want to take the ideas on, they can; but if they don't, that's okay. It's about cultural exchange and learning how you might work in humanitarian engineering.

PP: **When you travel to a country like Cambodia on a trip like that, do you travel lightly?**

CJ: I do have carry-on and checked [luggage]. I don't manage to do it without checked, but I'm certainly aware of only packing what I need to. Especially a place like Cambodia where I have a good understanding of what's going on. I understand how easy and quick it might be to do laundry or what pieces I might need and how often I might need to change them … and how quickly something might dry if I choose to rinse it in the bathroom. It's also about being able to be more mobile. So, the less I'm packing, the easier it is and the more organised my packing is, the easier it is to manage.

PP: Talking about organised packing, I believe you use packing cubes. What are those?

CJ: I love my packing cubes. There are a few shops that sell them. They've been around for a while. They come in different sizes. It's like a little … it's almost like a pencil case for your clothes.

PP: How do you use them?

CJ: They come in different sizes and I put different things in different-sized cubes and in the different types of cubes and different shapes. And when I'm feeling very organised I will colour code. They come in different colours, and if I'm travelling with my kids and my husband, and we're trying to make all the packing work together, I might put all the same … like it might be that T-shirts are in the blue ones, for example.

♛♛: What's it like travelling with young children and using the packing cubes?

CJ: It's easier with the packing cubes. I can roll up my clothes or their clothes quite tightly and small and line them up in a cube, zip it up … and it's also easy for them to be able to get their own clothes, that way it can be said, 'You need to go get a T-shirt to put on, go look in the blue cube in your bag.'

♛♛: Do you consider colour coding per child, so one child would just get blue and the other child would just get green cubes so that they would know which are theirs?

CJ: I would, but my two kids—despite being three years apart—are almost exactly the same size. I would certainly consider using one colour each, but I just don't have enough cubes of the same colour.

♛♛: What's travelling with small children like?

CJ: Um … hilarious! They're the best community engagement tool. I travelled to Aceh when my oldest was nine months old, and I was out talking to a community about relocation after the tsunami. It was the best way to get engagement and real connection with the community and talking to them about their experiences when I could pass a small child around.

You meet more people, I find, when you're travelling with small kids, because people on the street, especially women in a market or something, will engage in conversation or want to engage with the kids, so you have more opportunities to connect with locals.

PP: **What about the practical aspects of travelling with children, like getting through airports or spending time on the plane? What's that like?**

CJ: Just cross your fingers and hope for the best!

PP: **What advice would you give to Planepack listeners or readers on how to travel light?**

CJ: If I'm using a cube, I might decide that I'm going to put two days' worth of clothes in one cube, as a way to cause myself to be economical in my packing, and that also means that I'm only pulling out one package at a time instead of everything going everywhere when I pull something out of my bag. I think getting a few different sizes [of cubes] and thinking about how you're actually going to function with this in the field, so to speak … that's one way.

I also use a type of cube that's waterproof that's meant for hiking, to keep things dry. I use it for clothes that need to go to the laundry and I find that can be really good too because it allows me to compress those clothes and they're not going to make everything else smelly as well, so if you're sort of in between locations and don't have time to do laundry.

How packing cubes help you and your children travel light

PP: **Some of my readers have asked me or have said, 'It's very, very hard to travel light if you're travelling between two different climates.' Do you think if you were using packing cubes you could separate with something for a warm-weather climate and something for a cooler weather climate? Would it be a practical approach if you had to complete both in the duration of one journey?**

CJ: Certainly. I would probably go with a colour coding option, yes. I would use some of my larger cubes for some of those bigger, warmer things. But I always think, layers; you can always layer. To be honest, when you're in a colder climate you probably don't need to wash all those layers every time.

You might not need that many extra clothes, because when you're in a hotter climate you're going to need to wash them more often, but when you're in the cooler climate you can have many of those layers. And, just maybe keep taking the inside layer off and moving all the other layers closer to your body.

How to have an awesome style following as a man

Adam Moore is an Aussie bloke, married, with young children, living and working in Canberra. But what's exceptional about him is that he is a fashion icon. And he has an Instagram following at the time of the interview of nearly 12,000 people. I had to know more.

I think Adam Moore is probably Canberra's most stylish man. Certainly, his Instagram posts are testament to that, with 11,500 followers. Adam, how do you do it?

Adam: Thank you. I don't think I can claim that title, but I'll happily accept it from you. I don't know, I just try and be myself, be confident in who I am, and put it out there for people to see, and show that I'm proud of enjoying fashion, and enjoying dressing up and looking after myself. It really seemed to resonate well with people.

PP: **It's terrific, and it really shows, but what I'd like to talk to you about today is travel, and specifically, how to travel light. How much travelling do you do, by the way?**

Adam: I've done a lot of travel in the past twelve months. I think I've spent about six weeks overseas or away from home on longer-term trips in the past twelve months, and then a lot of weekend trips. I've got family both down the coast, on the south coast, and my hometown in Wagga Wagga, so we do a lot of travel, a lot of weekend trips to them, as well. So apart from just that six weeks, yeah, most weekends we're heading off somewhere.

PP: **Was your packing experience light, and could you describe yourself as a light traveller, or maybe let me ask you, how lightly do you travel?**

Adam: I definitely try and travel as light as possible. I have a wife and a son, and of course with a two-year-old, a toddler, you don't always get to pack light for them, because you need the essentials, so I find that the lighter that I can pack, always helps with making it easier on arriving at the destination, and getting home. So I am definitely what I would consider a light packer, as much as possible.

PP: **How do you decide what to take with you? What's your process?**

Adam: I guess there are a couple of things I consider, and that is you have to consider the time of year, which makes a big difference. Certainly, it is easier I think in the summer, to pack a bit lighter. In the winter when you are wearing heavier fabrics and layering a bit more, you tend to carry a bit more clothing. Well, I definitely do.

And also, you need to consider what you're travelling for. So if I'm travelling for work, I will tend to have a suit or at least a suit jacket and pants. If it's a bit more of a casual trip, just to see some family, I might not have those items. I might go a bit more casual, which makes it a bit easier to pack light as well.

PP: **What's your packing list? Do you have one, or would you be willing to share one with the Planepack listeners and readers?**

Adam: I guess I do have a packing list that I tend to go through; I'll start with the basics, which is obviously underwear and socks. Always have probably an extra one or two pairs of those, which I do take. I normally travel with a pair of chinos and a pair of jeans, and I find having one of each of those is really versatile.

I've got a really good pair of raw denim jeans from an Australian company, that I've had probably for about four or five months now and I still haven't washed them. That's the way you look after raw denim, you try and avoid washing as much as possible. So to have something like that in your bag, that you don't have to wash, that you can rewear, is excellent. And chinos I find really versatile. So whether I'm going away for work or for casual, a pair of chinos and a pair of jeans—a dark-wash jeans—are always in there.

With my tops, I'll normally have a couple of basics. I try and keep my tops really basic, so I'd normally be looking at a plain black and a plain white T-shirt, because you can wear them casually, but if you need to dress them up, they still look really great with a blazer. Depending on the time of year and what I'm doing, I'll normally have some type of navy blue blazer with me, or a suit jacket that can double between a more casual but, you know, if I want to go out for drinks or dinner, I can throw that on and look nice. Or if it is a work trip, it can serve as a suit jacket, something a bit more formal, a bit more businesslike.

And then in terms of a jumper, I try to be really picky with my warmer clothes. Pretty much all my warm clothes are 100 per cent wool or 100 per cent merino wool, so they're a bit lighter, they breathe really well, they don't hold smells. They hold up to hot and cold weather really well, so I'd normally take one or two jumpers, depending on the time of year. My wife says you always have to have a jumper with you, so even if it is summer, I'll tend to pack a light jumper. So that's my clothing, and I really will keep it light. For a weekend away, depending on the weather, underwear and socks, probably two pairs of pants, a couple of shirts and a blazer or a jumper, depending on where I'm going.

I'm always really careful to pack toiletries as well. My wife's a really big believer in natural skincare, so I always carry some natural skincare products, some moisturiser, some night cream, some eye cream … If you are travelling, especially if you're staying in hotels, you want your skin to feel good. You don't want to feel like it's dried out. So I always try to pack some skincare, just some moisturiser with some SPF 30 or SPF 15 sunscreen in it, just so you can look after yourself, and you don't come home and feel like you've got the dry skin. Then you know you can get ready for the week again.

I guess that's my pack, yeah. Some simple but good quality toiletries and some simple, basic clothes in classic colours and styles.

𝒫𝒫: **What about shoes? You haven't mentioned shoes?**

Adam: Yeah, so shoes. I'm definitely a real fan of quality leather shoes, so whether it's a leather sneaker, a classic white sneaker that you can wear with jeans, or really simple brown or tan boots. A Chelsea boot is probably my go to, where they go most places. I probably don't leave home without some type of Chelsea boot in black or brown.

If it's summer, I've got a few different loafers that I will wear, sort of that more Italian-style loafer. I just picked up a beautiful pair of green suede loafers, so they will probably be my go-to pick for this summer. I think a loafer for summer, and a boot for winter: you can't go wrong.

𝒫𝒫: **Can you tell us a little bit about what kind of bag you use to pack?**

Adam: I have a leather weekender that I picked up at a local market, probably two years ago, just a leather classic weekender, two zips on the end and a zip in the middle.

I'm a big fan of travelling cubes. I bought travel cubes; I got some from Kathmandu and some from Amazon. I'm a real fan of being organised, so I pack my clothes into those packing cubes, roll them down, pack them into cubes, and then I find that I can use space efficiently. Once I've worn something, if it's dirty or if I need to wash it before I wear it again, I've got a travel cube that I take with me for my dirty clothes. I try to remain as organised as possible while I'm away, and that way I sort of know what I've worn and what I haven't, and what I've got clean to wear if I need to wear it again.

PP: **What sort of techy stuff do you take with you?**

Adam: I'm a bit hit and miss with tech. I carry my phone, obviously, 24/7. I have a work phone that I take with me to most places, so I can get some work done if I need to. And we carry an iPad with us, which is does double duty, sort of: for us if we want to use it for anything, but also for my son, it comes in handy in the car if we're stuck in traffic or he wakes up while we're travelling, to put something on for him to watch.

Apart from that, it's a Kindle, which I don't travel without. The Kindle's probably my number one piece of technology. I'm a big reader and I find that having that Kindle with me, whether it's reading before I go to bed, or if I'm stuck in transit, if I'm flying somewhere, the Kindle's my number one go to. I do love a paperback or a hardback book, but I don't have space for it any more, so the Kindle's just a lifesaver in terms of being able to read and have multiple options to read while I'm travelling.

PP: **For sure. Planepack is all about travelling lightly, and what you've described sounds to me like it could qualify for light travel, but do you ever wear your**

contents, and have you ever considered travelling with carry-on luggage only, for a longer trip?

Adam: I think travelling light and travelling with carry-on only, I haven't gone outside of my comfort zone yet. It's probably something I need to look into a bit more, but it's definitely something I want to get into and I want to do more trips with carry-on only. Especially if it's more than a weekend away, I want to get into that, and I guess that's why I look at Planepack and follow the website to get those hints and ideas, but I think that will be my next adventure.

When I do travel away for more than just a weekend, it'll be carry-on only.

I've done it a few times, when I've just been away for a couple of days at a time, and I love that feeling of getting off the plane and just being able to walk straight out of the airport while everyone's waiting at the baggage claim. I think, definitely, that's where I'm going to be next time.

PP: **One of the things that you didn't mention about your wardrobe is a hat, because here in Australia, we really need to protect ourselves from the very, very harsh sun. So do you have a hat or something that you wear on your head?**

Adam: A hat's probably one of the key pieces of my wardrobe that I'll be umming and ahhing over for probably my next big purchase. At the moment, no, if I do travel, I tend to take just a baseball cap with me, and travel with that, but I'm really looking at picking up a timeless piece.

I'm looking at one of the Akubra range. The Akubra Stylemaster is probably in my sights. I think once I get the approval from the wife, that'll be the next purchase, and it works well, both for travelling, no matter where you're going away, or if you want to wear it to the races as well, it's a beautiful piece to wear. It's a bit of a statement piece.

PP: I really love the fact that you promote Australian designers and stylists and clothes. Can you comment a little bit on that?

Adam: I think growing up and being interested in fashion, and then really getting into it in the past four or five years, it's some of those Australian companies and Australian designers that have just really come onto the scene and marketed themselves as wanting to take Australian fashion to the world, and wanting to promote Australian produce, whether it's Australian wool, or Australian tailors, and that kind of thing. It really speaks to my heart.

I was born in Wagga Wagga, you know, not far from Canberra, and I really want to support local businesses. They're taking it to the world, in what they're doing, and they're producing some of the finest goods, whether it's clothing or footwear or hats. So I try and support

Australian-made and Australian-grown wherever I can, and that's something I'll probably always do.

PP: If you were to give a word of advice to a young man who's interested in following in your footsteps and dressing in a fashionable, and maybe classical fashionable way, what would your advice be?

Adam: I think my key piece of advice for everyone—and this is whether they're a young person and they don't have the budget to spend on clothes, or if they do have the money—for me, it's be confident in what you're wearing, and the key to that, for me, is fit. So if you're going to buy something, spend the five or ten or fifteen dollars to take it to your local tailor and get them to check it for fit, whether that's getting the sleeves cuffed up a little bit, or your pants just tapered a little bit to fit you a little bit better. I find once you've done that, you feel so much more confident in what you're wearing, and once you feel confident, you're going to want to wear it more, so you're going to get more use out of it.

So if you are on a budget, buying something and spending the money to get it tailored to you, you're going to wear it more and more, and eventually your cost-per-wear is much lower, rather than buying something and then only wearing it once or twice because you don't feel comfortable in it. So if you are on that younger side and don't have the money to spend, don't worry about going out and buying the most expensive thing.

Buy what's in your budget, but get it tailored to fit you. I think that's hugely important and that's one of the things that really made me more comfortable and more confident in what I was doing.

_PP_: If you had to name one piece in your wardrobe that's your favourite or your all time go-to, what would that be?

Adam: It's a really hard question and it's probably going to surprise people. I probably can't split it, but I will say I have a favourite … the pair of jeans I spoke about earlier, the raw denim jeans in the dark wash, they've been a staple for me over the last four or five months. I love them because you can dress them down casually, which is a surprise for most people, because if they see my Instagram page, I'm a bit more known for that formal-suited style. They've been worn a lot over the past four or five months, so they're my key.

But I also have a blue suit, it's a royal blue suit, and it's actually a cheaper one, and people are surprised to hear that because it is one that I've gone and got tailored. People are just amazed by it when they see it. They love the fit on me, they love the colour, and I always get compliments on it, but it's actually one of the cheaper suits, and probably the cheapest suit in my wardrobe. So it's probably those two pieces. Yeah, a royal blue suit that I wear a lot, that you can see on my Instagram page, or just a classic pair of dark denim jeans.

PP: **Adam, I could carry on talking to you. I'd love to know more about colour, fit, style, texture, fabric, but as the focus is really on light travel, I think I'll bring the interview to a close. But it would be really, really nice to collaborate on something down the track, and maybe we can come up with a line for men who wish to travel light. On behalf of Planepack and our listeners and readers, I'd really like to thank you. It's been fantastic talking to you. Thank you so much.**

Adam: Thank you for having me, appreciate it.

ADAM MOORE – MEN'S STYLE
Instagram: @a.d.a.m_moore

Cycling solo a thousand kilometres across Europe

Hans-Jörg is a science teacher, a university educationalist and an adventurer. He recently travelled solo across Europe by bicycle. I discovered that he's done this a few times; I was intrigued to know more.

PP: You recently travelled across Europe on a bicycle, tell us why?

HJ: I enjoy covering distance with my own muscle power; the flexibility of being able to stop and go as I wish, the flexibility of being able to reach places which I wouldn't be able to reach unless I had some sort of transport of my own. On holidays, I don't really believe in cars, because number one is that it's too expensive and number two, you end up traveling past things. OF course, you can reach destinations which I can't easily reach on the bike, but I like the control I have over my destination and about how much ground I cover. Walking is too slow for me: a lot of people like walking, but I find it's too slow.

PP: Where did you go on your most recent trip?

HJ: I have a friend in Florence whom I had wanted to visit for a long time, so this last trip was really just a thousand kilometres. From somewhere in the south of Germany across the Alps, across the Apennine Mountains into Florence.

PP: What are the challenges for you for such a trip, particularly considering you went over mountains on those long distances?

HJ: You always carry gear with you. For this one I tried to go as light as I could. I didn't carry any sleeping gear, I didn't carry a tent, I didn't carry any cooking gear. I just carried my clothes. I only had panniers on the front, not on the back wheel so I wasn't too heavy, and of course I chose the easiest route across the Alps, which was up a river called Inn that runs through Innsbruck; and you keep going and very conveniently it just rises and rises and rises up into the mountains. You barely notice that you are climbing until you are near the source of the river and then all you need to do is ride down into Italy.

PP: As easy as that? You just free-wheeled down the hill?

HJ: Yeah, very steep. Along the river there are always cycle paths. And going down on the other side into Italy, they have a few cycle paths, but you know, I also found the Italian motorists have a worse reputation than they actually are.

PP: What sort of goals or travel distances did you set yourself for each day?

HJ: Usually I go about 70 kilometres a day unless I feel particularly good and I want to cover more distance. I might stop at 60, but I usually try and not do less than 60 kilometres a day. It could be anything up to 150 kilometres; just based on how I feel, or in this case where the accommodation is because I needed to book ahead. I never book in advance; I just book on the day.

Carrying a smartphone, you always have access to various websites where you can on the spur of the moment find out what's nearby, what you can book. I usually stop about four or five in the afternoon and see what's nearby, where could I stay.

***PP*:** **In terms of covering those distances and traveling quite far, how did you sustain yourself in terms of your diet? What kind of food did you eat?**

***HJ*:** Usually what I do—again, it doesn't really matter where I travel—I try and have a good breakfast. I don't usually stop for lunch. I certainly will have a few stops, snacking and drinking all the time, and then I go till dinner time. If one is available I will then go to a restaurant. I will always have energy food in my bag that sits on the handlebars; snack foods, you know, like that.

***PP*:** **For the bike enthusiasts, did you use any kind of gadgets or devices to log your journey, measure your speed and your distances and things like that or isn't that part of your trip?**

***HJ*:** I can't even imagine going without a GPS and there are of course a number of GPS devices available for cyclists. I always—sometimes the night before, sometimes weeks before—I will plan my route, download it to the GPS, and I carry a laptop computer as well and follow that, especially where you want to follow complicated routes and avoid major traffic. It's really not practical o do that with a map.

You need to know exactly where you are going and you need some device that tells you, 'now, next turn, off to the left, and then go down that dirt road for one kilometres and then turn right onto the footpath' … and things like that.

I remember cutting across the country once a couple of years ago in northern Italy where of course there is the river plain and so many, so many roads available. To navigate that with a map is time consuming and error prone, but to have a GPS sitting there, it is just fantastic.

PP: **You have cycled with your son. What was that like? What's it like to travel with other people?**

HJ: With my son I have done shorter trips, but the big trip we did in 2013 was with my brother and that was in a ten-week trip through Scandinavia and the Baltic countries and Poland. It's a fantastic way to travel, I think again because you are not sitting in a car next to each other all day. You of course stay in the same accommodation—if you sleep in a tent, ideally everyone would have their own tent—and then you have breakfast or meals together, breaks together but then you are on the road and sometimes one is a kilometre ahead of the other one.

𝓟𝓟: **You don't stick together?**

𝓗𝓙: You can, sometimes you do, but it's very flexible; however, if you feel like you want to have a conversation you do that. If not, if you have had enough and you don't want to talk to your brother for a week … which also occurs.

𝓟𝓟: **I imagine if you are traveling on a bicycle that you need to be a light traveller, but you also have to take certain things with you. So how does it work? What did you take?**

𝓗𝓙: You need to provide for a range of different conditions. That starts with the kind of footwear you take because you want to have footwear that's suitable for bike riding even in wet weather. You want to have some shoes that you can use when you are walking; maybe you are in a hotel occasionally, so what you wear then? So you might already even think that you might want to take two or three pairs of shoes, for instance.

Regarding other clothes, of course the layering is really the thing. Isn't it great? People take many different layers and then you just put them on as you need them. Of course, you need to consider packing enough warm clothes for when it gets cold, and it does as we have seen in Europe just recently. My brother, who is currently cycling you know, told me that he was cycling in thirteen degrees in summer, which is the same climate you have in winter and so you need to provide gloves, and you may even need a number of pairs of gloves because it might be raining.

As you develop your experience, you then realise the kind of things you need for all sorts of different scenarios; I remember in Scandinavia when we were cycling I had bought myself the largest size of dishwashing glove I could find, so that I could fit my hand inside that with a normal pair of gloves and then the dishwashing gloves are over the top; because if it rains, no matter which gloves you have they will get dirty.

PP: **How do you fit everything you need onto your bike?**

HJ: Bike panniers.

PP: **What is a pannier for someone who might not know?**

HJ: It's a bag [like a saddlebag] that clips onto your rack. So you have got two of those in the back and two of those in the front and then you have got another bag that sits across your handlebars. You can really easily fit in a lot of stuff: we are talking about travelling light and I think that is not so much a concern for a long trip. What's of concern is to travel as lightly as possible while still taking everything you need for this kind of a trip; that involves, of course, your camping gear, sleeping bags and everything. It may be pyjamas or something like that, sleeping bag, sleeping mat, which in itself can already weigh fifteen kilograms.

PP: Did you take your bicycle with you from Australia to Europe? You put it on the plane?

HJ: I put it on the plane. I have got a bike suitcase, so I put my bike in that. My bike is quite heavy, because it's rated to carry up to 160 kilograms. Most bikes are only rated to carry 115 kilograms. I could easily carry 60 or 70 kilograms of gear in addition to myself.

PP: What advice do you have for someone who is considering going on a bicycle trip?

HJ: Nothing much really: you need your panniers, you need to buy all of that. Then really fitness, people say you need to train and be fit, but I don't believe in that. I think you just take it easy and as you then progress from day to day your fitness level increases and you are fine. The saddle is a big deal. People think, 'I need a soft saddle' and there is nothing more wrong than that. You need a saddle that can mould it yourself to your backside. I feel, when I climb on my bike and I sit on my saddle, like I have arrived home: it feels like I am comfortable on a chair. When you look at it it just looks like a torture instrument but it's nothing like that. So really that's important, to buy yourself a good saddle:

leather, plain leather is best—there is a firm in England that makes them, they are called Brooks. They are not cheap but they are the best.

The worst that can happen is you have creases between yourself and the saddle and then of course just avoid blisters. Some people buy pants that are padded: I have got a pair of those as well. Other than that, you know, people need to be comfortable and safe riding a bike.

PP: **What was the standout memory of this last trip that you did?**

HJ: Standout memory of that . . . of every trip, the standout memory is the enjoyment of riding on my own. I could say I even prefer that because it's an incredibly meditative experience. I remember I always used to think initially that you ride and you have thoughts going on all day, but nothing like it; there are no thoughts out there, you're totally immersed in the moment and just enjoying every bit of it. Occasionally a thought comes but not much. I have that every time and that's why I love it.

PP: **It's been delightful to hear your insights about cycling through Europe by yourself; thank you.**

HJ: Thank you.

How to brave the winter cold as an 'en plein air artist' and travel light

Josie is an artist and light traveller. She recently visited outback Australia with an *en plein air* painting group. This is how she met the challenges of art, travel and freezing winter nights.

PP: **You recently went on an *en plein air* painting group tour. What exactly is *en plein air* painting?**

Josie: Well *en plein air* painting is painting in the outdoors; travelling around to various landscapes, to capture the different light of the day, depending on how long you are staying in one place, any one time. It's a very good way to capture the colours and the mood of a particular landscape, more so than painting in the studio from photographs or drawings.

PP: **Painting outdoors: it sounds like a real challenge. Some of the things that I think of immediately: What about insects? Or what about rain? What happens to the paint?**

Josie: The challenges are really for oil painters because of the fact that canvasses take a long time to dry, so if you are thinking of doing *en plein air* painting you are best off to concentrate on drawing and watercolour media because they are very transportable, easy to set up, have a quick drying time and the paper is less bulky to transport than canvasses.

PP: **What is your medium?**

Josie: Well I do paint in oils, but for the purposes of this recent trip I did take watercolours, and that's good for capturing the colours and the immediacy of the landscape before you. I have found it was easy to pack them flat in the bottom of your bag or, with certain papers that aren't too stiff, you can roll them and carry them in a tube if you need to.

_PP_: Tell us about this group tour: what was it and where did you go?

Josie: If you are a painter you will be aware of just the plethora of trips that are available to you. In the art magazines that are on the shelf—*Australian Artist* and *Artist's Palette*—there are so many painting trips advertised and they are not only within and throughout Australia, there are also many overseas in Italy, Croatia, France—you name it, you can do a painting trip pretty much anywhere you choose to go these days.

_PP_: Where did *you* go?

Josie: Now, my trip I didn't find through one of these magazines, I found it through a fellow artist whom I had known through having an exhibition at the Belconnen Arts Centre where I sometimes spend a bit of time and she organises very small group tours of about 14 artists—not necessarily restricted just to artists, we have photographers who come along and we had on the last trip one travel writer, for instance. But the thing about going with a small group of like-minded people is that you are all cross-fertilising ideas about techniques and colours and you have a bit of a critique at the end of the day, which is all very rewarding in terms of getting as much out of the exercise as you can.

PP: How did you travel? Was it a tour?

Josie: This particular trip set out from Alice Springs in the centre of Australia; we travelled there by air and joined the tour which was run by Oz Tours Safaris and they operate with four-wheel drive specially modified trucks. They are not buses, they are trucks, and they are like the TARDIS; they have got everything imaginable on board and cater to all sorts of situations including all of your camping gear, your chairs, your tables to eat your meals from. They are just an amazing thing to see unfold and unpack.

PP: It sounds like it is a combination of touring and camping. Where did you sleep?

Josie: Well it was called the art tour and primarily this tour focused on following the Heysen Trail [named after Australian artist Sir Hans Heysen] down through the Flinders Ranges ending up at his residence and studio in Hahndorf, and so we did a bit of touring as well as stopping and painting at sites.

PP: Are you a light traveller? How did you manage with the luggage? You mentioned rolling up your

artwork or putting it at the bottom of the suitcase. Was there a choice to be made between taking clothes or taking artworks? Did you have a separate bag for the artworks?

Josie: Yes there were lots of choices to be made on this trip for me and I have to say that I would have spent four weeks considering all the items that I was going to take on this trip because the Oz Tour people like you to only carry a bag that weighs 12 kilograms. Now I myself failed because I couldn't get down to 12, I could only get down to 19 kilograms.

PP: Why 12, why was that the magic number?

Josie: Because it had to be in a soft sided bag, 12 kgs that would stack in the back of the truck above the fridges in the . . . if you can imagine the closed-in ute tray, there was only a little bit of shelving above the fridges . . . there might have been a couple of luggage racks but the bags had to be stacked on top of each other (the reason for being soft-sided) so no protruding wheels to damage other bags or the handler, who had it down to a fine art.

PP: So were the people's bags in one truck, or was there a range of trucks?

Josie: No, one truck. It was 16 bags by the time you included the hosts and the driver.

PP: **How cold was the trip?**

Josie: It was colder than expected because we had been watching the temperatures and they had been mid-20s for the two weeks before we left. Being Alice Springs in the central part of Australia you are thinking that you are heading up to a little bit of warm weather in winter, but it wasn't to be, it was the coldest start to winter that South Australia had had for some time and by the time we got to the camping part of the trip it was -4 overnight in the tent. So because we hadn't packed for any cold weather it was basically down to putting every layer of clothing that you had brought with you on for the night. Some people had the forethought to bring woollen socks, wearing their hiking boots. So that saved them. We were several, hundreds of miles away from any shops but the Oz Tour people did have hot water bottles on their truck.

PP: **Did you have to take your sleeping bag?**

Josie: Yes, they were on the trucks, the tents, the sleeping bags, the stretchers, you did have to put up your own tent up and your own stretcher and sort out your tent yourself.

PP: **How long did you spend at any one place?**

Josie: Well it was quite difficult getting the balance right in that regard; with only 12 days to cover the 3000-odd kilometres that we did, it was very hard to spend more than two nights in one place because we had a deadline to make and that was a little bit of pressure on the trip. Mostly we were one night, then paint during the day and travel on to the next destination, but on the days that we did stay two nights in one place it was luxury really because we got undivided painting time without having to worry about getting home and packing your bag and moving on.

_PP_: So what are the benefits of traveling light for this kind of a trip?

Josie: Well the benefits are that you get on the trip in the first place because I think if you turned up with a 23 kilogram suitcase it would be frowned upon. And the four-wheel drive variety that you get these days doesn't work in the bulldust let me tell you. So there is a benefit of traveling light with a bag that would be suitable to be used as a backpack, for instance, so that you can actually carry your bag on your back over the gravel or stone.

_PP_: What sort of a bag did you carry?

Josie: I carried a Samsonite High Sierra: it's a backpack but it does have two thick wheels at the bottom and it does have a pull out handle so it operates as a backpack, it's soft sided, has lots of different compartments which I found extremely useful and where I could in civilisation wheel it and in airports. I didn't ever carry it on my back because I had another backpack which I took with my painting gear in and that was the one that I carried on the back.

𝒫𝒫: So you did land up taking two bags? Was one bag for the painting materials and the other for clothes and toiletries?

Josie: Yes. One bag, the one I took on my back was specifically because I was doing a couple of little light tours before I started the main tour and so what I did and found very handy to know and avail myself of was to be able to use the hotel storage. So when I arrived in Alice Springs I repacked into my small backpack and did the two- or three-night trips and I stored my big bag at the hotel and came back and repacked for the tour.

𝒫𝒫: What was the whole experience like for you?

Josie: Well I was just completely blown away by how the outback landscape affected me and I thought that at the end of the tour I could have straight away turned around and gone back. I spent a lot more time out there and I just felt that some of the things were a bit rushed in that timeframe and there were some places—like, for instance, Hermannsburg which I didn't actually make it out to. That was a bit of an omission on that trip, especially as it's the home of Albert Namatjira and we currently have a fabulous Namatjira exhibition on at the National Gallery of Australia right now.

_PP_: What are your tips for somebody considering a trip like this?

Josie: Well I think a very valuable thing is to look at some of the lists or information that's available out there, both online and in magazines, from other people and other artists who have done the trip. They would have the packing down to a very fine art and I found those sorts of lists to be quite useful. There are only one or two things that were extra to what I would normally take on a large trip, for which I always have a checklist to make sure that I have got everything included that I need. So I think lists and drawing on other peoples' experience is important.

_PP_: Should you consider the climate variances if you are going in winter?

Josie: Yes, that's right. Although they can be unpredictable as they were on this last trip that I did and you know, we got rain at Uluru (Ayers Rock).

_PP_: What did you get out of the actual painting part of this trip?

Josie: The main thing for me was gathering reference material. I did some quick studies during the day when we had the time. I did a few drawings and importantly I took more than 2000 digital photos. So the reference material is invaluable for when you get back into your studio situation and you can still draw on that as well as the mood and the feeling that you still have fresh from the trip.

PP: **Those digital photos don't take up any space in your luggage, do they?**

Josie: No, no, but to be fair one of the heaviest items that I had to travel with was a camera.

PP: **You used a digital SLR and didn't rely on an iPhone?**

Josie: I took a telephoto lens, which was most essential for bringing back good reference material, but that was heavy. We made the decision when we took it away on our first overseas trip that it was way too heavy and that we would downsize to a smaller camera. For this trip I thought I couldn't get away with the limitations of the smaller camera for what I needed. So that was one of the heaviest things, and adding the charger and the batteries, spare battery and so on, there is a little bit of paraphernalia tied up with that. So if you can work around that somehow and still manage to get the sort of quality of photographs that you need, other people probably don't bother so much with that. They are just happy to make do with the paintings that they did on the trip and not work them any further.

PP: **For major research?**

Josie: No, but my dilemma was that because I work in oils the paintings that I did out there were mainly just studies to be worked up later in the studio with oil paints.

PP: **I want to thank you for sharing your trip with us because there are not many people who have an opportunity to go on an *en plein air* group tour to the heart of Australia. Do you have anything on closing that you would like to add?**

Josie: Oh, I am sure I could add lots of things but maybe we could do that afterwards.

PP: **Over another cup of coffee!**

Josie's trip essentials for specialised travel
- a small shoe horn for hiking boots
- battery-operated torch, clock and alarm (there is no electricity in remote areas)
- headlamps, which can double as tent lighting
- power pack for charging phone, etc, where there are no powerpoints
- three sizes of backpack; two that are ultralight

- down jacket that folds into its own hood
- thermal underwear
- woollen socks
- zip lightweight packs for undies, T-shirts, socks, chargers and other cords
- cabin pack for toothbrush, comb and underpants
- a sturdy 2 litre water bottle: you must carry water with you at all times when travelling in outback Australia

How to dress for comfort, style and light travel

Sonia Burke's range of light, quirky and casual clothes suit the traveller who likes to cruise. You can wear her tunics as you stroll the deck, or dress them up for dinner at the Captain's table. And best of all, they roll up into next to nothing to pack into your carry-on bag.

PP: You are a textile artist. Tell us about your Silk 'n' Things products. What are they?

SB: My product range at the moment is really about women's fashion. Fashion for women of more mature years. I think that as we mature, our body shapes change, and I don't think that fashion houses necessarily accommodate that change in our bodies. They don't cope with it very conveniently for us, so we're looking for garments that are comfortable, fit us well, and are stylish.

PP: Can you perhaps describe something? The top you're wearing, can you describe to the readers how it looks?

SB: All of the garments are, as I said, designed for comfort, so they're fairly loose fitting, long in line, and I use fabrics that are soft draping and easy care.

PP: Actually talking about fabrics is easy, so how do you source the fabrics, because when I came to your house to see the clothes, I noticed a real range of textures and fabrics?

SB: The textures, fabric, and colour are my forte, and I source the majority of my fabrics through shopping trips to Sydney and Melbourne. I'm very fortunate that I have contacts where I can check out the end of designer rolls, so my fabrics aren't necessarily available from regular fabric stores, which gives that uniqueness.

𝓟𝓟: **How and when did you start your business?**

𝓢𝓑: I've had Silk 'n' Things for about 24 years, but when I first began I actually worked with masses of silk, but silk ribbon. I was the silk ribbon embroiderer, and I handpainted silk as backgrounds, etcetera, and the over the years I've gradually progressed into other things of textile design, primarily because with the embroidery I was rather concerned that I'd develop RSI, so I thought I needed to do something that used my machine a lot more and not my hands as much.

𝓟𝓟: **I noticed you don't even have a website? Where do you sell your products?**

𝓢𝓑: Can I just say first off that I used to have a website, but I closed it down because the one thing about my clothing range is that every single garment is a little bit different, and as a consequence to operate my website, I would be endlessly taking photographs of the garments, so I found that I have a big enough following for my satisfaction to sell at the Old Bus Depot Markets in Canberra each Sunday, and then I also take part in special-event type activities, some in Sydney and some in Canberra and Wagga.

PP: **I came to one of those. I would call it a house party, which I thought was fantastic. It's really a lovely sort of safe and friendly atmosphere. How often do you hold them?**

SB: Well, to tell you the truth, this was my first one. Because I'm in this beautiful brand new home.

PP: **So it's a party for you as well as the other people?**

SB: Well, yes, and it was to, I suppose, allow all my friends and their friends to come and see what I'd been talking about.

PP: **What did you do at that house party? How did you manage? What was the process?**

SB: My main thing was I had to do lots and lots of pre-work as far as designing and stitching, which I did over the winter to have my new spring range ready for my friends, so I did lots of sewing, but to let people know about the event, I simply went through my database, so I personally emailed friends, and they passed on to their friends.

PP: **So it went viral in a small sort of way?**

SB: Well, yes. I gave out lots of flyers to people that I knew, and then spoke with regular clients that I have at the markets as well.

PP: I liked the way that you exhibited the clothes. There were, if I remember, three or four racks?

SB: Three racks, yeah.

PP: So there was plenty to choose from, and we were able to browse, and of course there were lovely nibbles as well and a great opportunity to meet other people; I thought it was a great formula. Were you happy with the amount of things that you sold?

SB: I was absolutely blown away. I really was. I think part of the success of it was that my friends brought their friends, and as a consequence, when women get together … magic happens. Someone puts something on, and then there's, 'Oh, that looks fantastic. Try this colour.' All that sort of camaraderie comes forward.

PP: Is this nicer than shopping online?

SB: Absolutely, because you have all this interaction, and on the day women meet other women that they hadn't known before, like I've met you. There's a whole lot of unintended networking as well, so we may see each other somewhere else, and I know it's you, Bobby.

PP: Would you hold an event like this again?

SB: Absolutely would. I've already had friends ask when's the next one. Maybe it was the bubbly!

PP: **I guess preparing for that sort of event takes, as you said, quite a lot of time and effort, and if I remember correctly, you produce all the clothes here in your house? You have a sewing room?**

SB: Absolutely. Yes, I design and sew all of the garments, because then I've got full control. That's how I can have each garment be a little bit different.

PP: **You mentioned to me that some of your customers love your garments, particularly those ladies that go on cruises. Can you tell me a little more about that?**

SB: I have a big following, particularly at the market, with ladies who are going away on overseas trips particularly—and of course many of them are cruising these days—and particularly my longline sleeveless vests, which they absolutely love because they're soft and draping, and they serve very many purposes. It's a very flexible sort of garment in that women can wear them during the day with a quite casual outfit, and it's just the little popover thing when the day might be a bit cool, when they go on their excursion and they first step off the ship for the day.

PP: **Can they wear the outfits when they stroll on deck?**

SB: Absolutely, when they promenade, but that same vest, they can coordinate it with a different top and soft pants or a longline skirt and wear it to dinner that night. Some different jewellery or a different undergarment and a bit of lipstick and off they go.

PP: **What about packing your clothes?**

SB: All the garments, all the fabrics that I tend to use are either noncrushable or crush very minimally, so they might unroll their garment and just simply hang it when they arrive at their destination, and within a couple of hours it's dropped out. But they all fold up and then roll into a small ball. Perfect for hand luggage when the aircon is a bit cold on an aircraft or in a bus or however they're travelling.

PP: **Would you say that it'd be suitable for light travel? I'm interested to know how much they weigh if you have any idea of that?**

SB: I've never actually weighed any of the garments, but they're very easily held in one hand.

PP: **Are you a light traveller yourself?**

SB: Over the years I've certainly become lighter. I don't know whether I would be an actual light traveller as in just a piece of hand luggage. Maybe if I was going to Sydney, but a six–eight week trip to Europe, not at this stage.

𝒫𝒫: But you'd be fully kitted out in Silk 'n' Things!

𝒮𝐵: Absolutely!

𝒫𝒫: Absolutely. Sonia, it's been a delight talking to you. I don't know if there's anything else that you'd like to tell the listeners about your clothes, promote them?

𝒮𝐵: I think probably the best thing is for them to come and see me at the Old Bus Depot Markets in Canberra, Wentworth Avenue each Sunday up until Christmas. I have a break and then I return in March.

𝒫𝒫: Thank you so much. It's been a pleasure talking to you.

𝒮𝐵: My pleasure.

FIND SILK 'N' THINGS ON FACEBOOK

www.facebook.com/Silk-n-Things-795593953831166/

How to ski those slopes as an awesome light traveller

Skiing is not a sport I know much about, but I found someone who does. As *The West Australian*'s accredited ski writer, Susanne Roberts contributed regular ski travel stories—a gig that took her to some of the world's best ski resorts.

𝓟𝓟: I believe that in January you're going to Canada for a ski trip. Why there?

𝓢𝓡: Canada is a great destination for skiers because it's welcoming. They understand the Australian sense of humour, unlike sometimes the Americans. Terrific snow of course, and lovely accommodation, bigger and more luxurious really than most Australian snow accommodations. And great value: lift tickets and ski hire, it's great value. We enjoy it a lot.

𝓟𝓟: Where in Canada are you going to?

𝓢𝓡: We're going to a resort called Big White in British Columbia, where we have been before. I think last time we were there we didn't see the sun very much, but there was lots of snow and we liked it. It's not one of the biggest resorts. The village is not one of the biggest, but the ski fields are terrific. And all standards and … I'm pretty sure we can be guaranteed great snow.

[Big White, Canada - image courtesy of Snowpak]

𝓟𝓟: How and when did you first start skiing?

𝓢𝓡: I was taught to ski by my father, a Swedish Army Officer, in the grounds of Drottningholm castle in Stockholm. Now, I don't remember that unfortunately but I do have photos so I know it's true and my brothers can confirm that. In those days, on wooden skis, straight wooden skis, because I'm quite old really, I'm in my sixties. When we moved to Australia, it took me a long time to get back to skiing, but for the past twenty-odd years, my partner and I have skied both in Australia, New Zealand and really all over the world. At least once a year.

PP: What is it about skiing that appeals to you?

SR: Well, anything covered with snow is beautiful, and it takes me back to my heritage really. It's fun. It's outdoors. Yes, it's cold but if you dress properly for it, you're not cold. And it just makes me feel terrific. It's a bit like yoga, really. You concentrate on what you're doing in your space and it's just lovely.

PP: You mentioned that you've skied in quite a few places around the world; what's your preferred destination?

SR: That's really, really hard to answer. As I come from Europe I do love the European cultural experience that comes along with skiing, but skiing in Australia this past season was terrific. Skiing among the snow dams on a good day is wonderful. Thredbo's great, Falls Creek, Mount Hotham, Mount Buller, just lovely. Perisher, great. We've skied in South America, even in Chile, and that was an amazing experience, too. So I think just wherever I go, as long as there's snow, I'm happy.

PP: Have you ever gone skiing at night?

SR: Not really, it's a big deal at some resorts and it's really mainly for families with kids who enjoy that experience. I mean, for one thing, at night it's colder. Children, perhaps, don't feel the cold as much as we do. I prefer at night to be having a good dinner, maybe some wine, rather than to go skiing.

I know a lot of people who do enjoy it. There are fireworks at some resorts, to sort of mark it as a special thing. So, yes, it can be fun I'm sure.

PP: I imagine that skiing is very dangerous. Is it dangerous for you?

SR: These days, with very good equipment and good instruction, you learn what to do and what not to do. I mean, as a beginner skier, you don't go on the more dangerous slopes. On one occasion—it wasn't at all on a dangerous slope it was at Thredbo—I don't know what happened, but I managed to fall and knock myself out and got carted off the mountain and had some short-term concussion. No pain or anything like that, and I was wearing a helmet of course, which everyone should be doing. But that did shake me up a bit, and I tend to be, now that I'm older, fairly cautious. I'm a cruiser, I'm not a racer, no downhiller, by any means. I just like to cruise around and make nice turns and enjoy nature.

PP: Packing for a ski trip, what's that like?

SR: Well the first thing of course is, if you're going overseas, leave your skis behind, because no one needs oversized luggage with them. It's far better to hire skis at the resort and then you can also hire according to the conditions. If there's been lots of fresh snow, you'll hire fat skis. That goes on the snow better than your normal old mountain skis. Take your own boots of course, because once you've worn in a pair of boots, it's a good thing for your skiing. No ski boots are comfortable, but your own that you've worn in are more comfortable than those you're going to hire. Of course, dress in layers. Good thermal wear is absolutely essential. And a good ski jacket and good ski pants. Jeans, of course. Forget about the high-heeled shoes or anything like that because you won't wear them. Wear good walking shoes with thick soles. Take a colourful ski jacket, which lets your partner pick you out from all the others on the slopes.

PP: Do you have a packing list to share with us?

SR: Well you start off with your ski gear: with your jacket, with your pants, with your boots, with your socks, thermal underwear and use the space in your boots to stuff your socks and your underwear basically. Take your boots in perhaps your carry-on bag; most boot bags are carry-on. Goggles, of course, and helmet will also, most of the time, go in your boot bag. Mine certainly does. They are pretty heavy boots, I think mine weigh about 3.7 kilograms. So, packing a boot bag as carry-on luggage, most of the gear should go in there. And then your après-ski stuff. I mean, you know …

𝓟𝓟: I've heard about this famous après-ski entertainment and social life. Please tell us about it.

𝓢𝓡: Well, it's not as glitzy or glamorous as you might think. You really dress warm and comfortable. Think about itting around tables having dinner or having drinks or something so, some detailing on your jumper, a bit of glitz on that perhaps is a good thing, but jewellery and things like that, don't worry about it. Very simple jewellery, if you take any at all. And of course, a beanie, and a good light down jacket and good fur-lined boots possibly, to get you around the resort, from place to place.

𝓟𝓟: What's your non-ski wardrobe?

𝓢𝓡: Most places are very well heated inside. So, you don't need overly thick jumpers. You need probably a thermal, a light jumper under a down jacket, possibly a neck warmer. A scarf if you'd like. And certainly a beanie. Beanies are actually really good for walking around, yes, but also, lots of places have hot tubs outside. Now, that's all very well and you're warm up to your neck, but put a beanie on your head and you'll be warm all the way through.

PP: **How long do you go for when you go on your international ski trips?**

SR: Well, some people stay at resorts for weeks and weeks. We find that we go for eight nights or something like that: that's enough. We've then been around the resort, been to the restaurants we want to go to and we've skied the place pretty well. So we tend to be pretty intense about that and ski every day, if we can, if the weather allows us, so that's really enough time for us.

PP: **If you're holidaying other than for skiing, are you a light traveller?**

SR: I do try to, on trips across country, back to Perth, for example. I tend to travel, if it's only for a few days, just with a carry-on. Especially in summer of course, with Perth's mild climate. In winter, I do like to have a couple of jackets and scarves, and a few changes of shoes, things like that. So, I certainly don't over pack. I try to be pretty economical and I match things.

PP: **What tips do you have for someone who's keen to start skiing?**

SR: Just do it. Go locally first, and if you live in the eastern states, obviously, there are terrific ski resorts here. Don't buy equipment, hire first and see if you really like it. The very first thing you must do is take lessons. No one is a natural skier, and you need to only take lessons for, say, five days. Ideally go for a week, take lessons in the morning, practise in the afternoon, and after that time you should be able to cruise around most of the mountain. Leave the black runs to later. Then just enjoy it, it's not an extreme sport really. Yes, there are kids doing somersaults off jumps, but most of us just enjoy getting around the mountain and stopping for coffee or hot chocolate and enjoying the view, meeting other people, and it's a really lovely way to have an active holiday.

PP: Do you have any other feedback you'd like to give to the readers and listeners?

SR: No, not really. I think Australia offers really wonderful opportunities for all kinds of holidays, so we're very lucky. We've got fabulous beaches and we've got really lovely mountains. And they are lovely in summer as well, of course. If you don't want to go skiing, go hiking, and enjoy the change of scenery and really beautiful nature that we have in this country.

𝓟𝓟: **Thank you, Susanne. It's been lovely talking to you.**

𝓢𝓡: Pleasure.

THREDBO ALPINE HOTEL, AUSTRALIA

https://www.bigwhite.com/

https://www.thredbo.com.au/accommodation/thredbo-alpine-hotel

How to care for the environment and be a light traveller

Maria Filardo is a Canberra architect, interior designer and light traveller. She's also an environmentally conscious and stylish designer and renovator of homes and businesses.

[Maria on the right]

PP: You are an architect and an interior designer. What does that mean?

MJ: I think the simplest way to explain it would be … Interiors do, obviously, just the internal parts of the building. So, if we're looking at this building here for example, I would do things like shop fitouts, bathrooms, kitchens; look at things like the layout of things of space; lighting of course would be another consideration. All the things that you sort of feel, look and touch is what you would do for interiors in addition to the layout for it.

For architecture, you look at the shell of a building, how it sits on site. Also, how it looks within a block, within a city. Sometimes you can extend beyond and then go into event planning as well, of architecture. The architecture is like a mass of everything, whereas interior design is more about the space internally. And, the two can blend together. And so what it means for my work is that I can do a complete building. I don't need to have anyone else look at the internals for me. I can do that. It's part of the package, which is I think is a more holistic way of dealing with a project and delivering for a client. And, I think it makes it a lot easier for them, rather than having to engage with different professions along the way.

PP: I read a recent article in *Homes Canberra* that stated you provide services from start to finish. They listed these as concept sketches, design,

documentation, council approvals, and interior designs. Which, for you, is the most challenging?

MJ: I think each stage has its own challenges, but dealing with councils has to be the most challenging. Simply because you're trying to deliver, for a client, a particular vision with their work and for the design, but then also you have a whole sets of rules that you need to comply with. And so, sometimes you need to break those rules, and it's a question of how you can try and massage your way, shall we say, through that to get a positive outcome for the client, but still then complies to a degree to council regulations. So, that can be a challenging component behind it.

PP: **Your portfolio ranges from residential architecture through hospitality, and even into retail design. I was drawn to your hospitality designs particularly RYE Café [Braddon, ACT] and Western Basement [Weston, ACT—since closed]. What was your brief for those?**

MJ: Oh, okay, so with RYE, the client wants Scandinavian, they wanted to put a Scandinavian feel. And, that was the basic brief for it. So, we just kept it very clean, very pure. A lot of white timbers was the approach. And, just also it was nice that it was a completely different approach to a lot of your cafés, which are going for the industrial look. Yeah, That was the premise for that café, which is basic Scandinavian, which was unique to Canberra, which was lovely. So, that was a great project.

And then, Western Basement … It was a while ago now. So, the brief for that was because it was a basement, they wanted it to feel sort of dark and dingy and it's a thing that you really … the entry points … there's a structure as you enter that's really compressing people that go down and enter the space. So, it's about really hardening that feeling. That was the main emphasis for that, and then just extending in terms of all the materials inside. A great deal of that was recycled. A lot of the furniture, for example, was recycled. The materials throughout were basically repurposed, which was really nice. There were very few that were just shiny and brand new in the space.

PP: **Can you tell us a bit about CBD butcher, Tom's Superfruits and Fruitylicious [all ACT retail]? They all look amazing in the photos on your website.**

MJ: Aw, thank you. So, with all three projects, they always come to the same request: 'We want a point of difference,' and 'How do you achieve that?' And, I think in retail there's a great shift in terms of the daggy feel. It just doesn't cut the mustard anymore. People think these days. Are a little fussier. So you really need to have an edge to things.

With the butcher, we took the approach of: let's treat this like a little jewellery box. It's something precious. Really, like I mean, these animals have sacrificed their lives for us. Let's just honour that in a beautiful little fitout, which is really what that was. So, that was our approach for that one, for the butchery.

And then, for Fruitylicious, that was something that's a little bit more artistic and more fun, and they have quite a colourful logo with that. Again, it was about displaying the fruit like they're works of art themselves, as well. Then hence, the displays being suspended in midair.

And then, there was Tom's Superfruits. And again, that was a fairly modest approach to it. Just revamping it without taking away the essence of this supermarket, because again it belongs in the market. They wanted it to be authentic and true. It was just like polishing the edges of it, to make it shiny enough for people to enter, to want to be in this space, but then not yet detract from what the body of that business was, and what clients know and love when they enter.

PP: **It's those lovely touches that make it worthwhile employing an architect. Our listeners might be wondering, what does architecture and design have to do with travelling light? Well, in my mind they're both about style and caring for the Earth. So, let's talk about the style aspect first. Where does your sense of style originate?**

MJ: I think, honestly, it's a combination of things. It's developed over time. It stems from: my education, what I've been exposed to, different art movements, different exhibitions that I've seen. It's all developed from there. Things that have really resonated with me. Just things that I've seen that look very beautiful. Beautiful detail. Or, the colour of something.

I think for me when I was a young student, the movement that really captured me was De Stijl, art by Piet Mondrian, and the thing that really stuck out was the simplicity of the lines, but also the bold colours. And then you just look further into the work of how they actually come together and it was all these mathematical equations, which formed the artwork to begin with. So, it's completely fascinating and then it just sort of goes from there.

PP: Why did you do interior design on top of your many years of study of architecture?

MJ: It made sense at the time to do that, actually. I thought the two complement each other. It's a skill that I know that I had. Comments were made by lecturers in terms of, you know, 'You have the skill. You have a talent for it. So, do it.' So, I thought, 'What's four more years? Why not?'

PP: Let's talk about caring for the Earth. As Canberrans, we appreciate our precious

environment. What do you do in your practice to uphold sound ecological practices?

MJ: So, the first question when you're delivering a project ... Let's just take something simple like a domestic renovation or extension. You ask the question, 'Why? And how much?' If you have a client, for example ... I think of a client in particular who were a couple and they have a couple of animals. And they had a three bedroom house, and the question was, 'Do you need to have a three bedroom house? While you live here, do you have lots of guests? If there are no plans of having little people running around, why do you need so much space?' Basically, because the more space you need, the greater the footprint on the Earth.

Then we have these horrible houses in these new suburbs that have no backyard, but it's essential to actually have a backyard and some beautiful greenery. And, not to just completely pillage the Earth with a built form. So, you ask the question, 'Why? How much? And, how big does the space need to be?' And just question your clients to push them. But, they'll give you a brief, but also to go, 'Well, how can we bring this in and how do you have spaces that are cleverer than that, than the norm? Do you need to have two dining rooms? Can we have one? You know, let's be clever with our storage.' Maybe ask your client to consider culling some of their stuff that they haven't used for years. That sort of thing. So something with a very basic approach of, 'Do you really need so much? Let's just re-evaluate. How about the quality of your life? Are you home so often that you really need this 500 metre square house?' The answer is, 'No'.

_PP_: I quote one of your clients, 'We never dreamed we would get a result to rival the glossy lifestyle magazines we have been reading. The final results blew us away.' How do you achieve this level of style while using sustainable materials? And, what are sustainable materials?

_MJ_: So, when it comes to sustainable materials, my philosophy is this: if you were to specify material that might be 'green' in inverted commas, but your client hates it, and in two years time they're going to replace that, how sustainable is that? So, you're better off getting a product that the client loves and that you know will sit there for a long time. That for me, is sustainable, because sustainability also goes beyond the environment. It's also about mental sustainability. Someone has to be happy in this space. They have to love being there. So, it's about putting things together to consider that. If you're talking about sustainability, timber can be quite sustainable because it's really the only renewable source that we have. But, you need to consider what application you have on top. Will it be glued to the floor? Will it be nailed? What finish will you have? If you have polyurethane, that's not sustainable at all. The best is to go for oil finish, because that's more natural. So, they're the sort of things you need to question then, with your client.

When it comes to joinery. You can have boards that have EO [ethylene oxide] emissions. So, you would make sure you specify that. Again, the finishes that you apply. Polyurethanes tend to be very high in terms of their emissions; there are better alternatives available. Not everything is to a client's taste. So, there are always some compromises to be made. But, again it's also about making sure that it's something that the client will love for a very long time, want to have in their house, and be durable. And, that for me, is a part of sustainability. Knowing that there's longevity there for that as well.

PP: **Let's move onto something closer to Planepack. Are you a light traveller?**

MJ: I am. Yes. The very first time I travelled, I wasn't a light traveller—I think like most people really. And, I just thought, 'This is ridiculous. You have to lug around all this luggage from room to room. It's a hassle. There's gotta be a better way.' And, the advice given to me as a student, the first time I travelled … I was advised by one of the lecturers. They said to me, 'Pack your bag, take everything out, and then put half back in. And, I promise you that's all that you will need and you can make do.' So, I did that and it worked, which was fine.

But then, my approach, things have been even more refined as I travel. So, I'll always have a little makeup bag with me, which has the basics: toothbrush, toothpaste, basic makeup, sunscreen.

And clothes, I'll always coordinate. 'I'm going to go for five days. What can I re-wear? It's not going to kill me. I'm not going to be filthy. Know what the weather conditions are going to be like. How can you layer? How can you make something smarter? I don't need to take 20 pairs of shoes. If I can do it in two or three, let me do that instead.' So, I think coordinating the clothes makes a big difference, because you don't have to have 20 things to accompany it, more than anything. Accessories change the look of something. Be clever and do it that way.

PP: **Is this the architectural approach to light Planepacking?**

MJ: Coordination is key.

PP: **What is your most important object, product or device when you travel for business?**

MJ: My phone. Simply because banking details are on there. All of my emails are on there, obviously. So, in terms of being able to communicate with people. I've got maps, of course, to get around. So, that for me is the most essential item.

𝓟𝓟: You can run your whole business from your phone?

MJ: Virtually.

𝓟𝓟: Getting back to architecture, what advice do you have for women who are considering architecture as a career?

MJ: Follow your heart. Really. Like, if it's a passionate thing, you've got to do it. So, don't let anyone put you off. I recall when I was a student, someone made a comment saying, 'Ah, you'll never get through. My brother failed it. It's a really hard course.' And, hearing that made me even more resolute to get through this course. So, yes it was hard, but it's worth it in the end. Because, when I wake up every morning, I want to go to work. I love what I do. Life's just too short to end up miserable in a job that you hate because someone else suggested that you should do that. Listen to yourself. Drown out those sounds, and go for it.

𝓟𝓟: Absolutely, right. Thank you so much. It's been wonderful talking to you.

MJ: Pleasure.

SEE MARIA'S WORK AT

https://www.feas.com.au/

How to travel like a man who packs lightly

James McPhillips and his wife Amy run Mint Content, an IT content writing and strategy business. They've lived in Thailand and work in Australia, Singapore and Europe. I wanted to find out how James manages his wardrobe, packing and carry-on bag.

PP: **I know you are a light traveller; you once sent me a photo of your bag. What prompted you to travel like this?**

JM: I first started travelling light in about 2009 on a trip to Europe and I just had a backpack—a very small, probably 20 litre, backpack—and I found that I was just so nimble, able to get through airports super quickly, and when my clothes would get get sort of dirty or whatever I would just throw my T-shirts away and buy new T-shirts in whatever country I was at. I found it was such an efficient way to travel. So easy, saved me hours inside airports and it was just the way to go with it.

PP: **When we talk about travelling light are we talking just about carry-on that you take onto the plane with you?**

JM: Correct: that's right. I basically refuse to travel with any sort of checked baggage nowadays.

PP: **How do you decide what to take with you?**

JM: I have sort of a system basically of what I pack. It's kind of changed over the years from early days of just packing a bunch of T-shirts and shorts and things like that and then for the summer months and then figuring out ways to keep it confined to a small bag or small wheel-on case that I have nowadays. And it's just evolved from there to get cleverer and cleverer with as much stuff that's actually useful to me on a trip, so it's all necessity, I think.

PP: Do you use a packing list? Can you share it with us?

JM: I do, I generally do, yeah that's right.
For sure.

PP: I know that you have been overseas for quite a long time, but if you were to travel with a carry-on bag like this, how long do you normally travel for?

JM: The trips I take vary; usually I guess the most recent long trip was almost a year.

I would pack a standard amount of luggage and then when clothes and things like that deteriorate I will just replace them while I'm there. I have kind of a sort of disposable attitude to a lot of the stuff that I pack, I guess. And there are all sorts of good, interesting antibacterial fibres and stuff like that, like shirts and stuff made of microfibre that pack up really tightly.

I think Tim Ferriss [from *The Tim Ferris Show*], who most people are aware of, he has got a good series on packing light and I think there are a lot of products and a lot of T-shirt fabrics and all of that sort of thing that he mentions in there that are really good.

𝓟𝓟: What does your partner think of this? Does she travel lightly?

𝓙𝓜: She travels not as light as me, but she has definitely come around to the concept of trying to get through airports [quickly] and carries as little as possible.

Does she travel with carry-on only as well?

𝓙𝓜: She does mostly. Occasionally I think she may have to check a bag or two if there are presents or things like that that she is bringing back but probably 80 per cent of the time it's carry-on only.

𝓟𝓟: Would you like to share perhaps some anecdote with us or tell us a little bit about what your travels in Asia were like; what did you like most?

𝓙𝓜: Sure. Well, I have been spending a lot of time in Thailand, in the city of Chiang Mai. It's been great for building a business because the cost of living is so low. Now anecdotes-wise I am not sure if I have one on hand but …

***PP*: Is it culturally different in terms of the things that you carry with you or the things that you might wear?**

JM: I guess for me it's probably because it's so warm there all year round, and that allows you to pack even lighter. Especially as a man, I think, you can get away with packing a lot less than a lady who may have to pack things like hair dryers, so I think men generally do have an easier time with packing light.

***PP*: What's your favourite bag? You mentioned that you used to backpack but now you have a roll-on.**

JM: I have upgraded to a roll-on small wheelie hardcase bag. I think it's good to travel with a hard case. Some way to protect it from just the elements and it gives the actual bag structure so you can organise it well, I think.

***PP*: Are you able to stay under that seven kilogram limit, which is mostly what you carry on?**

JM: Generally yes, probably the heaviest thing that I carry with me is a laptop that I usually keep in a laptop bag with me. I have also found, too, that if your bag does go over the limit—it depends on the airline—but if your bag does go over the limit they are often amenable to a bit of negotiation and trying if you can sweet talk out of a fine or whatever the extra charges that they put on.

_PP_: What's your advice for someone who may be considering traveling light?

_JM_: My advice would be to think of your packing or think of what you take as just the necessities. I suppose think about what your week or something looks like inside a foreign country and how often you will be able to wash your clothes, for example. Things like that and just be very pragmatic, don't take anything that's . . . unnecessary. You need that minimalistic sort of lean traveller mindset to be able to do it, so then it's so much easier, it's so worth it.

_PP_: What's your top tip for somebody who wants to travel light?

_JM_: Good question. Don't be afraid to throw away clothes when you need to, or put them in a charity bin, if there is one there to make your life easier I suppose.

_PP_: That's great, thanks James, it's been wonderful talking to you.

_JM_: No worries.
Mint Content: IT writing, strategy and marketing

How to travel like a pro for three months and two seasons

Rebecca Blackburn is an environmentalist, science writer and a seasoned light traveller. She shares her tips and her wardrobe for travelling three months at a time across seasons and climates.

𝓟𝓟: **You've been travelling light for almost ten years now. How did that all come about?**

𝓡𝓑: It probably all started when I moved to the UK and started travelling regularly. So, off on the weekend, I'd go for a couple of days. And, it was just convenient.

𝓟𝓟: **By travelling light, do you mean with carry-on only? No hold luggage?**

𝓡𝓑: No, no. Just one wheelie bag and one crossbody handbag.

𝓟𝓟: **How do you plan for a trip like that? Let's say you were going to fly off tomorrow, how would you plan for your wardrobe? What would you take with you?**

𝓡𝓑: So, it depends on the season. But there are a few set, standard items that I take. Let's start with the sustainability aspects. I would take my Klean Kanteen, which is a thermos, a drink bottle. You can put your tea or coffee in it. It stays hot or cold and it's your cup as well, so that's number one. And I also take a folding purse, a little handbag: for any shopping, for a beach bag, your laundry bag, it's useful.

Clothes-wise, I take layers. A lightweight jacket, like a japara trench coat that's waterproof and windproof. So that's your top layer. And underneath I have one or two wool layers. Possibly. I've just discovered the ultralightweight puffer jackets.

𝓟𝓟: Is it tiny?

𝓡𝓑: I know, packing it comes down to 10 centimetres; it is tiny and it also doubles as a pillow. So it's super-warm and windproof as well, so that's another warm layer. And then, other essentials are a pair of leggings, 'cause I always wear those. You can wear them for sleeping; as your warm layer under jeans, if it's really cold; and also, and if it's ultracold, I wear a tight pair of thick wool knee-high socks. And then a pair of jeans.

𝓟𝓟: Is there something else you would take with you to dress up?

𝓡𝓑: Yes. I take a ponte blazer—a stretch blazer—that looks smart and it's comfortable. I would take scarves: scarves are gold. They add colour and can be worn in multiple ways. You can wear them as a sarong; you can use them to keep you warm; you can wear them to just add colour. And you might find one or two quite useful. I also take, for going out, one dressy top. Lipstick and some flashy earrings. And I also take one pair of dark coloured trousers or jeans.

It doesn't really matter that you might be walking shoes on the bottom. But, because people don't really notice: what they notice is your face. They notice whether, you know, you're wearing a bit of makeup, whether you've got earrings on, whether you, you've got a bit of colour. That's what they notice.

𝓟𝓟: Absolutely. That's the message I like to get across to people as well. Because shoes are heavy.

𝓡𝓑: Yes.

𝓟𝓟: What shoes do you take with you?

𝓡𝓑: Yes. I take a pair of smart walking shoes. And, if it's summer, I would have some, either Birkenstocks or I actually quite like Ecko as a brand.

𝓟𝓟: For walking shoes?

𝓡𝓑: For sandals and walking, I have a pair of black patent leather Ecko sandals. So, the patent leather dresses them up but they have a cushion sole. Because if you're walking for ten hours a day, you do not want a flat pair of sandals.

𝓟𝓟: You need comfort, don't you?

𝓡𝓑: Yes. And so with shoes, Ecko also do leather lace ups. Some of them are daggy. You do have to sort through them and find some of them are a bit more fashionable. But, there are lots of other brands too.

PP: **Yes. I like that idea of being able to combine day shoes with your evening gear as well. So you don't have to take an extra pair of shoes for dressing up. And as you said earlier, no one ever notices what you've got on your feet. In fact, nobody ever notices what you're wearing when you're travelling.**

RB: Absolutely. I mean the main import is to be comfortable, to feel that you're protected from the elements, and they're the most important things. It is nice to not look too touristy.

PP: **What is your carry-on bag?**

RB: Actually, I can't remember the brand, but it's just a hard-case wheelie bag. But it fits, I checked before I bought it, that it fits the airlines about, I think it technically doesn't fit Ryanair, which is the cheapest airline in Europe. And I have an extra small size. But they never, ever questioned it, I might add. I like that it is a hard case because it's robust and it has wheels, and I can lock it.

PP: **Yes. And the carry-on allowance is seven kilos. Have you ever been turned back from your line and told oh, your weight is too heavy, you've got to put it in the hold? Or do they generally accept it?**

RB: No, I haven't been turned back. You do have to be careful because even with a bag of that size you can go over the weight. Don't take books. Take a tablet, an e-reader. I don't take books.

PP: **What about cosmetics or toiletries, because they weigh quite a lot. How do you manage those?**

RB: I did take a miniature set with makeup. It's just lipstick, foundation, mascara and eyeliner. Really, really basic. Oh, and I have a lip gloss as well.

PP: **What's the longest period that you've managed to travel with this constrained wardrobe?**

RB: Three months. I travelled all over Europe and it was four seasons. So, I started in Portugal and then went to Morocco in September, which is really hot. And, so, I had swimmers and summer dresses. But then, by the time I finished, it was December and it was in Paris and it was crazy. Literally close to zero degrees.

PP: **How do you manage travelling through seasons?**

RB: Your bottom layer is like T-shirts and your cotton leggings. And a summer dress. And then you add: fine wool is fantastic because it's warm. if it's really cold, the puffer. And then your japara or trench coat that you wear over the top. You do need a hat, gloves. On your legs, you wear jeans or leggings plus knee-high socks, which I discovered in London: the fantastic knee-high wool socks really make a difference because your jacket will often come down to your knees. But then you need something from your shoes up.

PP: **If you're wearing a coat like the one you mentioned, not the puffer jacket. Would you take that with you on the aeroplane, so that it's not packed into your carry-on bag? Or is it part of your carry-on pack?**

RB: I would carry that on the plane.

PP: **What are the benefits of travelling light?**

RB: I would never, ever go back. So, when I was eighteen, I went overseas—well, maybe I was nineteen. I went overseas for the first time on my own and I took a pack. A big bushwalking pack. And it, when I remember when I returned it was like eighteen kilograms. And I'm petite—I'm about five foot tall—I could barely carry the thing. It was utterly insane. I cannot understand why I did that. And, now I've discovered travelling light, I would never, ever go back again. Because it's easy, once or twice we've had to run through airports ... For my last trip to China, exactly that happened. I didn't put luggage into the hold. We had to make three really tight changeovers. And I was able to do it because I had carry-ons.

𝓟𝓟: What about negotiating trains, buses, boats, cobblestones, lifts?

𝓡𝓑: It's so much easier because it can be quite awkward. I will say, wheelie bags are not great on cobblestones.

𝓟𝓟: But you can you pick it up and carry it.

𝓡𝓑: You can pick it up and carry it, yes. I also have a carry-on backpack.

𝓟𝓟: What kind of backpack do you have?

𝓡𝓑: With a zipable frame. So it all just zips into one neat little parcel. So I use that for kinda like rougher, adventure travel because it's easier to shove into small spaces.

𝓟𝓟: If you had any advice from someone who wants to change from carrying 20 kilograms in the hold to travelling light, what would you say to them?

Rebecca: The first step is planning. So, lay out all your clothes. Do this at least a week before you go. And, everything you take's got to go with everything else and it's got to be multipurpose. If you've got something that's a single use, it's a complete waste of space, is basically what I would say. You want things that can layer on top of each other, dress up, dress down.

PP: Is planning essential?

RB: Yes. And, honestly, if the worst comes to the worst, if you miss something, you can usually buy it. In fact, some people—and I'm starting to think this way too—with an umbrella, why bother? There's no point in bringing an umbrella because usually when it rains, especially if you're a tourist, the instant it rains, suddenly out of nowhere, these people appear and they'll be selling you an umbrella. The coat or jacket, yes, but the umbrella, no.

PP: It's been fantastic talking to you, Rebecca. Thank you so much for your time.

How people make life after rugby more meaningful

Planepack talks to Clyde Rathbone of Karma.wiki about letters, living tributes and life in general. It is people, he says, who enable him to live a meaningful, well-travelled existence.

PP: **You started an organisation called Karma [karma.wiki]. Can you tell us a little bit about that?**

CR: Sure, yeah. It's a project my brother and I have been working on for a couple of years, and Karma really is an online platform that builds on meaningful human connection. What that actually means is that it's a place to write about other people, about the people who have made a positive impact on your life. We've seen long-form letters on Karma to mentors, teachers, even communal letter events where friends and family come together and write a stack of letters, and then publish them on a major life event, like retirement or a birthday or a birth or wedding. The feedback we've got from recipients of these letters is just phenomenal. People constantly reach out and tell us that's the best gift they've ever received, so that's the underpinnings of Karma. We wanted to create a place that was different from other social networks in that it wasn't all about you. It wasn't all about the individual. It was about others. It's been an interesting journey.

PP: **When I looked at Karma, I saw that gratitude is the sort of cornerstone of the site, so what do you, personally, have to be grateful for?**

CR: Oh jeez, so much. I think the fundamental things are almost clichés, but they're known as true for being clichés and that's friends, family, my health, living in a beautiful part of the world, just having work that's in perfect alignment with my values. Every day I wake up, and I'm excited to go and work with my team on something that I think we all feel is bigger than any one of us, and just being able to build something. There are no definitive answers to how you make a success out of a start-up, and that's what makes it exciting and a worthwhile pursuit. So all those things, but, fundamentally, it's the relationships with people that I'm most grateful for.

PP: Clyde, you were a formidable and dynamic rugby player. What did you learn during that career that informed your decision to start Karma?

CR: It doesn't seem like an obvious transition from sport to the tech world, but I think the thing I learned most about life from rugby was what matters. When you start out in a sport as a young person, you're very focused on some of the quantitative stuff—how many games you play, how many tries you scored, how much your contract's worth, all that sort of stuff—but if you stay in it long enough, I think, by the end of your career, if you've paid attention, you realise what actually matters are the people and the relationships you form and the shared experiences and memories that you take with you long after you've hung up the boots. So going into Karma, I was weighing up what to do with the next phase of my life. It was important for me to do work that really aligned with what I think is important. I'm very lucky to have found that.

PP: As you mentioned earlier, it's about the people, and it's interesting to hear that that's kind of the main ingredient that you got out of this long and illustrious career. I'm interested in packing, of course, and staying with rugby, I'd love to know what is it like to travel and pack as a rugby player, and who carried all that gear?

CR: Yeah, it's crazy when I think about it now because you take an enormous amount of stuff with you all around the world, and most teams have what's known as a 'baggage master', because of what a big job that is, and his role is to coordinate with the airports. We have, obviously, a huge amount of oversized stuff. Individually, you've got a lot to take because you're taking training gear that you're often changing three or four times a day because you've got different training sessions. You're taking a whole array of different rugby boots. You have all your formal stuff for post-match functions. It's kind of an obscene amount of gear when I think about it now and a huge undertaking for any one person to manage, so it's nice not having to worry about it.

PP: I know you travel a bit for Karma. Are you now a light traveller?

CR: Oh, much more so. I think it's just easier to be able to throw everything into one bag and know you're set for the whole trip. I almost view it a bit like minimalism on the run. One of the best things I've done in the past few years is really simplify my life and get rid of clutter and owning less things, but things that I really love. I think travelling now, trying to have a similar mindset. You don't actually need half the stuff you think you need. It's just a kind of different conditioning. I travel much lighter now.

PP: **When I heard you speak about Karma, and before I even read the letters, I got a sense that you and the organisation are all about travelling lightly through life, and you kind of touched upon that in the earlier response about minimalism. Can you comment about that?**

CR: Yes, I think that's a really good insight. I think it's about being more mindful about what matters. A Karma letter is really an opportunity to clear your mind of clutter and just meditate on someone who's made a profound impact on you, and that practice, I think, it flows into a lot of other things. All of a sudden, you start to become mindful of things. Do I need all this extra stuff? Is it just getting in the way? It's one of those cliches that you start to be owned by your things, and I think that's true, and I think Karma as an organisation really is about less but more quality. You could think of it by juxtaposing Karma with a Tweet. A Tweet is

140 characters. It's very odd for that to contain much value. It's particularly hard for it to contain value that's persistent. A letter is long-form, really considered thoughtful content that is going to be valued deep into the future. Many generations from now, people will be able to read those letters and get value out of them.

𝓟𝓟: What's been the reaction of your friends, family, and colleagues to your making this move to Karma?

𝓒: It's been great. I think it's obvious when someone's doing work that's the right fit for them, and I'm lucky that a lot of the early adopters of Karma were friends and family. My background—I come from a writing family. My grandmother was an author … is an author, I should say! She's in her late 80s now, but she's still writing. My mother was an English teacher. A lot of my friends read, so I think the idea of Karma appeals to that inner circle, and these were our early adopters. From there, it's expanded out, so the reaction's been great. The support of friends and family has been … it's a big part of how you make your start-up succeed, it takes a village.

𝓟𝓟: You've lived and travelled through a few interesting decades in your life. You retired in your late 20s first, and now in your mid-30s you're in charge of a start-up. How will you travel into your next decade? What do you see for yourself?

CR: That's an interesting question. I think there is so much left to do with Karma. We're a couple of years in, but we're really only starting now to scale and go to the next phase, and that's going to demand a lot of time and effort and concentration, so I think the next period is going to be very much focused on building this company. But also, I'm looking at starting a family next year, so that's going to add some colour to the mix. It's an exciting time.

PP: **What advice do you have for listeners to travel lightly, both literally or figuratively?**

CR: The thing, literally, is actually to plan the trip, so look at what you're going to be doing, and when in doubt, take less because you don't want to be in a situation where I've been on, where you've got three pairs of shoes, and you only wear one over the two weeks you're away. You're wondering, 'Why did I bring these?'. I think it's a little bit of forethought.

Figuratively, I think it's just to take the time on a daily basis to meditate on what's important and why it's important. I think, when we do that, most of us arrive at similar conclusions. What's important are people and the journey that we're all on and understanding that we're all in it together.

PP: It's been wonderful talking to you, Clyde. Thank you very much.

CR: Thank you. It's been great.

How to save time by travelling with light luggage

Robyn Pearce is a time management consultant and business owner. She's a mother of six, a successful author, a business traveller and an all-round wonderful woman. I spoke to her in Auckland from Canberra.

PP: You've got a business called 'Getting a Grip: Helping You Find More Time'. Can you tell us a little bit about that?

RP: I've been a time-management specialist, helping people with work–life balance, productivity, and all of the topics that come under the loose umbrella of time management, for about 25 years. People often say, 'How the heck did you get into something like that? Did you know there was such a career?' And my answer is always, 'Because I was always trying to fix my own problems.'

PP: You come across as being very organised. You haven't always been like that, I gather. How did that come about?

RP: Well, there's two parts to that answer. In fact, I was always very organised, from a very young girl, with stuff. My first career was as a librarian. So I've always enjoyed putting things in order and having them lined up nicely. And some people would say I was anally retentive at a very young age, which is probably true; however, my time skills were a different kettle of fish altogether.

I have raised six children, one of them an intellectually handicapped foster son. And they all came in a nine-year period, and life was really crazy. I was married to a farmer at the time. Life was just ... I don't know ... it was chaotic actually, would be the right description for that.

And it wasn't until some years later, I got the marriage break-up and I was by that time living in Auckland and selling real estate, and one day having a pity-party with some friends on Sunday morning, moaning and complaining, because I didn't have enough hours in the day. And this friend said, 'For God's sake Robyn, go and get a decent diary.' That was the beginning of the journey.

PP: **And that's how it all started?**

RP: Yeah, it did actually start just that way. I had started learning my ... putting my own life in order, until one day a couple of years later, a friend said, 'I've got a coaching client who needs to be helped with his time management. I think you can help him.'

I was very shocked and said, 'Me? You know how I'm always late for things.' But she had seen something in me that I hadn't seen in myself, and so often that is the case, isn't it?

And of course, if you're teaching somebody something, you're reinforcing that habit yourself. I'm a walking proof of that.

PP: **I read your article, 'Travel Light and You'll Save Time'. It sounds like you're a Planepacker through and through. Can you tell us about your travel packing habits?**

RP: Well they have simplified over the years probably. Actually I'll tell you a really funny story that's not a Planepack story. Just to help explain why I went this way: in 2000, I did my very first really long distance haul to England with my daughter.

I'd been in America for a conference and then I went to England and travelled round England with my daughter who at the time was about 23 or 24. The grandchildren had started coming along—not her children but her brother's children—and they wanted some LEGO. So in my wisdom I had bought a bucket of LEGO actually in New York before we went to England. For the rest of the three weeks or four weeks that we were tootling around England I was lugging this bucket of LEGO as well as my bag. At the end of the trip I just had no idea about simplifying things. I had a big backpack—I'd thought that would be the way to go—that had cost me a fair bit of money. I had this wretched bucket, and I had another bag that I bought to put the overflow of things in. I so did not know how to pack lightly or to travel lightly.

I have been working since then to simplify and then over the years I've made more mistakes. But now yes, I just love travelling with a carry-on bag in the cabin, not in the hold.

PP: **In the spirit of finding more time, how would you say that packing lightly helps?**

RP: It's enormous. I've just been in America and a little bit in Canada but mainly in America for the last four weeks not very long ago. I really noticed the contrast. The friend I was travelling with had a big bag and I could run up stairs where the friend was all lugging a bag. He took such up far more space in his part of the bedroom than I did. I just took a little bit of space. I could pack every day, three times faster. I could unpack and sort out what I needed. Just in every respect it saves something much time because you're not faffing around making choices, having to keep things clean etcetera, etcetera.

PP: I like your comment in the article, and I quote you, 'Don't dress to impress.' Can you tell us what you mean by that?

RP: Once upon a time when I was packing I would look at my wardrobe and I would see all the nice clothes that I have bought when I'm at home and I'd think, 'Oh it would be nice to take that one. It'll be nice to take that one,' so I would take the clothes to be more fashionable.

Then I began to realise, the rest of the world doesn't care. They are only looking at you in that moment. You might be with friends for a short period of time but even so, it's rare that you're travelling with those same people day after day. If you are, they don't care because they're trying to pack light as well. Or if they are bringing fashion items, well they will be the one with a big heavy bag and I'd rather be the non-heavy bag person.

PP: As a business woman, who needs to take work materials with you, how do you see yourself minimising that in the future?

RP: I've done quite a lot of it; I'm not sure though there is much more that I can reduce. When I'm travelling my office now is just a backpack, and usually it's a very small backpack. In there I've got my laptop, and I've deliberately chosen a smaller laptop so I can use it on the plane if I want to, plus it's not as heavy. I've got the charger obviously, I have my phone, I have the charger for the phone and I have an iPad.

Now the reason I take an iPad as well is that that's my books. I now download eBooks. I can remember some years ago being in France before we started using much in the way of electronic books and I found myself getting very anxious when I was running out of English material. Although I'm studying French, I'm not competent enough to read for enjoyment in French. So the iPad is my choice. Now I know there are lighter devices. It could be possible that I go for lighter. It's possible that I could be reading a book on my computer but the laptop doesn't hold as much charge and I just like the size of the iPad for reading so I've got Kindle for iPad on it. You're probably going to suggest I get something smaller.

PP: We all love to read a good book and you mentioned Overdrive. Would you like to tell the readers about Overdrive?

RP: I would love to tell the readers about Overdrive because there's no need to be buying books all the time. Part of the simplicity is not being unnecessary consumers. My local library put me onto it initially and it's available—it's an app basically—right throughout the world and it's connected to whatever library; it would be a very small library that wasn't involved with the process. But it gives you the ability to read ebooks. Now, there is an app that comes with it and I would suggest, and this is new (I only found this out last month) there's one called Libby, L-I-B-B-Y, and that is part of the Overdrive function but it's an app rather than the slightly more clunky way that you had to get at it.

So check out Libby in the app section you'll find as part of Overdrive. It means that you can be reading on any device and it synchronises immediately with wherever you left it off.

PP: That's wonderful. It's a big saving because I've noticed even Kindle titles are creeping up in price. So being able to download for free, borrow them effectively, is fantastic.

RP: Another one of those time-saving things, Bobby, while we're on books is that in my phone, I keep a list in

Notes—now you could do it with Goodreads, I haven't got clued in on that one yet but I believe you can do it—but in my phone in Notes, I keep a record of books that I would like to read. So I now keep a separate list of books I'd like to recommend, having read them. So I'm never short of suggestions of something I might want to read if I'm somewhere where I've read all of the things that I currently have in my Kindle. But I will say that when I'm at home I read physical books. I'd rather read a physical book but I don't want to carry them.

_PP_: If you had one piece of advice for someone considering light travel or making the transition to light travel, what would that advice be?

_RP_: You share so many really good tips on your website already. But there is something that I have learnt the hard way: when you go to put something in the bag just in case, you don't need it. Take it back out again.

The other one I would add is, start thinking about it and perhaps lay it out a few days in advance. So that you've got everything out before you start putting things in the bag and then adding in the last-minute things. It's better to have everything there and look at it. Give yourself time to think carefully about how little you can get away with. Because what I find is if I leave it too late, I'll end up throwing things in because I haven't got thinking time to think in a minimal way.

PP: **The preparation is as important as the packing?**

RP: Yes it is. It's giving yourself headspace so that you can think minimal, rather than thinking, 'I might need it.'

Exactly. It's been absolutely delightful talking to you. Thank you for being a pioneer, talking intercontinentally with Planepack. I do appreciate it. Thank you so much.

RP: My pleasure Bobby. Thanks for inviting me.

GET MORE TIPS ON TIME MANAGEMENT FROM ROBYN

www.gettingagrip.com/

How an internet scientist navigates astonishingly frequent business travel

Geoff Huston, Chief Scientist at Asia Pacific Network Information Centre (APNIC), is a self-confessed 'geek who speaks' and regular world traveller. His talent is in revealing complex scientific and internet issues to the layperson. Geoff presents on these complex issues at international internet conferences. He took time out of his travel schedule to tell me about his travel experiences.

PP: **You are the Chief Scientist at APNIC, which is the regional internet registry serving the Asia–Pacific region. Can you tell us a little bit about that?**

GH: It's always a tough job to explain, but in essence we are one of the so-called infrastructure folk in the internet and our job, bizarre as it sounds, is to hand out internet addresses to various internet service providers—the folk you get your internet from. But it's sort of a little bit more than that because the rules and the framework that we work with are actually built by the community. This is sort of industry self-regulation so we and our sister organisations around the world regularly meet and regularly discuss what the internet needs at a particular point in time and how we can create mechanisms to distribute addresses, that are fair and equitable but also meets the needs of the industry. We don't all go to one place all the time; being community-based we tend to go where people are and so that does involve a reasonable amount of travel one way or another. So, yes, in my job I do a fair deal of travelling and meeting folk as well as working on the infrastructure of the internet.

PP: **Some time ago you mentioned you travel at least once a month. Is that correct?**

GH: Well, you know, two of my friends, we have had this discussion. We have talked about cutting down, and cutting down means once a month. Typically the load can be a lot higher; either the trip gets longer—the last one I did was four and a half weeks—or you are doing around two and sort of badly three a month depending on what the travel is. So I think for the first five months of this year, I did six, seven trips; something like that.

$\mathcal{PP}$: Where do you go when you travel?

$\mathcal{CH}$: Now literally it's where folk are meeting so I started the year with a trade conference in Hawaii and then off to a technical meeting in New Zealand. February I think I gave a talk in Hong Kong and then off to a conference in Ho Chi Minh City. Somewhere there was Chicago and New Orleans and so on.

$\mathcal{PP}$: There is a certain amount of anxiety and stress associated with travel. How do you deal with that?

$\mathcal{CH}$: Well it varies by the trip to tell you the truth. Some trips are astonishingly rewarding; you sit there and think, 'Well, that was absolutely brilliant.' At one point we had a meeting in Phnom Penh and a couple of us scooted off to Angkor Wat for the weekend before and you know Angkor Wat is one of those places that once you go there it's just overwhelmingly beautiful. I think that was a great trip. I went to Chicago earlier this year and it was still in the depths of winter; it was grey, it was raining, the wind was absolutely horrible and it has this subterranean system and I think I spent the entire week down in this rat's maze at the bottom of Chicago. I didn't see much else: I could do without that kind of trip. So it varies a lot. This latest trip I have been on I was in St Petersburg and I have always wanted see the Hermitage Museum. It was really a ball, not the least of which is once you have done your talk and met folk, you can run away—and the Hermitage is one of the nicer places I think in the art world to run away to. So those kinds of trips make it worthwhile.

PP: **Are you a light traveller?**

GH: It varies a lot and it varies on the range of places you are going to and the season. I don't travel with suits. I have done it in the past. It's a minor inconvenience; I don't have any formal or business wear. So I tend to do the whole jeans and shirts and not much else. So generally light. If I am going into the depths of winter—like Chicago in March is a depth-of-winter kind of country—I would travel with more gear than if I am going somewhere in their summer. So it varies a little bit, also the hassle.

PP: **Talking about the hassle, do you travel with carry-on luggage only or do you put stuff into the hold?**

CH: I normally have around 12 kilograms. If I get someone tough at the local desk, 12 kilograms can't be taken on board the first leg. I can either book to Sydney, retrieve it and go onto the next leg or decide, 'ah stuff it,' and send it through. I think we are lucky in Australia. Certainly there is no surcharge on my business travel for putting luggage in the hold. When I travel on the American domestic legs where everyone has got this massive surcharge—you know, 25 bucks a piece—that's enough to convince all of them to attempt to take it on the plane. Because if they knock you back they can put it in the hold for free. So you have this massive amount of luggage. I tend to look at what airports I am going through because taking all your stuff in a carry-on can kind of stop you when you are getting through tougher places.

PP: **What do you mean by that?**

CH: Heathrow is tough.

PP: **So taking a carry on is . . .**

CH: Well, I carry a lot of computer gear so it is lots of cables and wires and if I compound it with all of my toiletries and everything else, invariably I am spending about 15 to 20 minutes going through the security, which is fine unless you have a—in Heathrow about a

45 minutes to one hour—changeover and if you have 45 minutes to 1 hour it's difficulty on carry on.

You put the entire thing in the hold and if all you are dealing with is a backpack it's a lot easier. So that's all part of the factor of a bit of luck with me. Will I just throw it on the hold . . .

PP: What kind of luggage do you travel with?

GH: I always travel with a roll-on and a backpack. The backpack carries all my computer gear: the laptop, the power supply, the camera, the iPad, power adaptors, cables and medicines. I never put medicines in the hold. And then the roll-on carries clothes. And shoes.

I try to avoid taking a spare pair of shoes. It really depends on the trip, but shoes take out time and weight. If I can get away with one pair, I feel good about that and, as I said, it depends on the length of the time. Once you are going for five days, you can go for ten weeks; it really doesn't matter.

PP: What are the essential things that you need to take with you when you travel?

GH: Well it's almost a routine; there is a certain stock level of clothing that is almost independent and then there is the optional outerwear, which depends on the season. So if I am travelling as carry-on I will take a thicker jacket or something that I can just hang off my shoulder; a little bag or something like it so I can put it on when I get there. I don't try and pack it in because they just get too bulky.

𝓟𝓟: I thought you were going to say that your cables, all your computer equipment is probably your essential travel gear?

𝓖𝓗: That always comes with me.

𝓟𝓟: If it were to get lost that would be challenging?

𝓖𝓗: Well my meds and computer gear and, of course, the laptop all travel in the same bag and that always travels with me; never goes in the hold. What goes in the hold—even when I lose it—is not a great problem.

𝓟𝓟: Has your luggage ever been lost?

𝓖𝓗: Lots of times. Generally it's been Heathrow and I think nine times out of ten it's a transit through Heathrow which I always find a bit weird. I did one trip Phoenix to Athens and it was Phoenix to Dallas, Dallas to Heathrow, Heathrow to Athens. The plane was late leaving Phoenix; Dallas I had to flit across the airport; it's a big airport and I thought I was the last person on the flight to Heathrow. Heathrow was a more relaxed 90 minutes to get onto the plane to Athens: that's fine, let's get on the plane Athens. Get there; no bag, but the bag was in Heathrow not Dallas and I was like if you are gonna lose it you're going to lose it on the tightest connection, but no, the Americans managed it and Heathrow was an epic fail. But as I said normally it's just clothes, which is an easy thing to fix unless you are in the middle of a holiday weekend.

𝓟𝓟: You mentioned previously an interesting story about the level of satisfaction?

𝓒𝓗: Oh yes, in terms of airline loyalty—the analytics firms have been into this a lot—the question is, what can an airline do that will increase your love and affection for them and your sense of loyalty? It seems that of all the experiences airlines can give you, recovering your lost luggage is the gold-star event and honestly it increases the level of customer loyalty and appreciation more than anything else they can do. If you think about it, British Airways must be really high on everyone's list because Heathrow is really the cemetery of lost luggage.

𝓟𝓟: What happens to all the luggage I wonder?

𝓒𝓗: Oh they don't want it. They eventually try to reunite you. The worst possible situation is when the luggage and its tag get divorced and all of a sudden the bag really has very little identification and then it can take forever. As long as the tag is on it—I remember talking to some of the folk about it—there is a loadmaster when every flyer is boarding and you can talk to the loadmaster if they've got the time. If they look at your bag tag they will tell you if your bag is on the flight because they know.

And it always annoys me that they only ever tell you, you are missing your bag once a) you've unloaded and b) if every last piece of luggage is unloaded. You wander off to the luggage office going 'no bag', but they already knew that hours ago.

You could have told me straightway and I would have waltzed through customs and walked away going, 'Find me later,' but no, it is a kind of a formal song and dance that involves about an hour and a half, which I find bizarre because they already knew straight away that you and your bag had parted company.

𝓟𝓟: Isn't it one of the biggest frustrations standing at the carousel waiting for your bag to arrive, and it doesn't?

𝓖𝓗: Well every person has a moment of anxiety and it doesn't matter what class you are travelling or how it's tagged, because it's the order in which the cans are unloaded and it's not even the tightness of the connections to tell you the truth. It's some random . . .

There is some luck of the luggage draw and a certain amount of mis-sorting. I arrived in Hong Kong once, on what I thought was a really ordinary flight, Canberra to Sydney, Sydney to Hong Kong. No bag and they go, it was routed via Perth and then that's kind of just misrouting right? It went the wrong way on the conveyor belt and there is nothing we can do about it. Most of the time, though, the lost stuff for me is at Heathrow ... not that I go through there that often but that's where all the loss events occur.

PP: **What is your advice for people who may want to travel light?**

GH: Firstly, see if you can wear one pair of shoes; leather, comfortable . . . that can take anything because shoes take an enormous amount of weight and size in your luggage.

Secondly, always remember that there are shops. You don't need to have one of everything, you need to cover 60 per cent of your expectation and if you really get caught out—miles too hot, miles too cold—buy it. I was down in New Orleans in May and I was in straight from Chicago. It was really cold in Chicago, but New Orleans was kicking mid-thirties I think: it was really hot. Fine, go and buy a pair of shorts and light shirt and then throw it out at the end; you don't need to pack for everything. Pack a lot less and remember no matter where you are on the planet there are shops willing to sell what you don't have.

Thirdly don't try and take too much paraphernalia: the portable speakers, the this, the that, the extra lens for your camera. All of that is size and weight and most of the time it's either on your back or you're lugging it and it's never used. My other advice is when you unpack at the end of the trip look at what you didn't use and don't take it next time. You generally find that if you do that about three or four times you are down to an extremely small set of stuff because that's what you actually use.

PP: **Excellent advice, thank you Geoff.**

GH: Thank you.

You can read … : do you think I should add this reference to Geoff's achievements?

You can read more about Geoff's achievements at the Internet Hall of Fame.

Melody: For all the articles, I'd like to reference
- the podcast
- the original post
- for the digital, embed the audiofile into the text (ePUB file)

See the links below.

Please advise what is the current url convention for print books: must we use the long url as below? It's so much easier for the digital edition . . .

For the digital edition, we can publish the call to action as the link.

How to become an evangelist for light travel? Join Planepack!

An interview with Planepack author and light travel evangelist Bobby Graham. Bobby describes her philosophy of travelling light with handheld carry-on luggage only.

Planepack: exploring the world

Fiona Rothchilds: **This is an interview on Sunday, 26th March 2017 in the Joplin room of University House at the Australian National University. I am Fiona Rothchilds, currently interviewing Bobby Graham of BG Publishers (aka Planepack). We are interviewing Bobby about Planepack travel light experience which is part of Bobby's latest venture. Welcome Bobby.**

BG: Thank you so much.

FR: **What is Planepack?**

BG: Well, Planepack is my philosophy of light travel and it's something that started off quite a long time ago.

FR: **When you say quite a long time ago, when was that?**

BG: Back in 1977, when I did my very first trip overseas to Europe I squeezed 14 extra T-shirts into my already bulging suitcase. When I got to Europe I realised that was a bit of a burden, so I posted those T-shirts back and I realised then the advantages of travelling lightly.

FR: **Did you travel economy class or business class?**

BG: I have only travelled economy class, I haven't been fortunate enough to travel business class yet.

How to become an evangelist for light travel? Join Planepack!

JR: What is Planepack to you?

BC: Well Planepack is a way of travelling lightly and enabling myself to be free to do quite a few things that I wouldn't be able to do if I was lugging a heavy suitcase.

JR: Is Planepack carry-on luggage or checked-in luggage?

BC: Good question: it's carry-on luggage. So since 2010, I have been travelling overseas with carry-on luggage only for all my long haul trips and during that time many of my friends have said to me or asked me, 'Bobby, how do you do that? You have to teach us how.'

JR: When you say luggage, what do you mean?

BC: I travel with a carry-on bag that is a standard small roll-on suitcase. Obviously if you like to travel with a backpack you can do that too, but the idea is that I only carry about seven kilograms of packed clothes for an overseas trip.

JR: That seven kilograms, does that include the weight of the bag?

BC: Yes indeed it does. If you are considering travelling light you need to find a travel bag that weighs no more than about two kilograms, and I personally like to travel with what's called a clam-opening suitcase that opens up into two sections, but those are little heavier than those that zip open and I am always on the lookout for light luggage.

JR: When you talk about carry-on, do you mean that you are putting your hand around a strap and lifting it yourself or do you mean that's it on coasters and you push it along?

BG: Well, the ones that I use—both of the bags that I use—have got wheels. So they are standard cabin luggage and they have to conform to the airlines' requirements: they have to be a certain maximum size. The options that we travellers have is in choosing the lightest one of those, but yes it's carry-on luggage; I don't travel with any luggage in the hold. In fact, the last few times that I have done that, whenever I stop over at an airport the stewardesses usually look at me quizzically and say, 'What, Mrs Graham, only hand luggage? No check-in luggage?' and I say, 'No, I prefer to travel lightly.' So it does require a certain amount of discipline to travel and enjoy a trip like this.

JR: When you talk about discipline, what do you mean?

BG: Well if you are planning—when I am planning—a trip overseas, let's say I am going away for two or three weeks, I like to visualise what I am going to be wearing and what I am going to be doing over those few days and what do I actually need to take with me. So I think the first principle of Planepack is that you need to carefully consider what is that I am going to be doing and what is it that I am going to be wearing, principle number one. Principle number two is to find the right clothes for those opportunities and occasions. Principle number three is to prepare carefully before you travel.

JR: **And then when you are travelling what do you need to remember?**

BG: Well I think the preparation and the packing helps me to plan appropriately so that I don't leave things behind. The clothing is obviously quite an issue; we, as women, all want to look nice and we want to be comfortable and happy when we travel, but I suppose some of things that you are alluding to are things like chargers, cosmetics, appliances, anything else that you might need for a two- or three-week stay away.

JR: **When we talk about chargers and adapters, if we are travelling into different continents what do we need to remember?**

BG: That's a good question, as each country has different power sockets. I usually buy or travel with an adaptor for each country so there would be a different one for

Asia, for Europe, for the United States, for South Africa. I usually just take one charger with me and one adapter with me and the one charger then has to do for all my appliances. The only device that I travel with these days is an iPhone.

JR: **When we talk about iPhones, tablets, smart-enabled technology, are there any matters that we need to consider if we are only taking in carry-on luggage?**

BC: Well my principle always is travel with the lightest possible, there is no problem with taking an iPhone on board, some airlines have instituted regulations these days that you cannot travel with an iPad on board and I advise travellers to check what those might be. As I said earlier my principle is always to travel light. Now in terms of what I do with my iPhone, I use it for everything while I am away. So I read my books, I watch my videos, I check my email, I check the internet, I generally use the phone for everything that I would do at home and I travel with good headphones and that's about it.

JR: **What is Planepack's philosophy in terms of mix and match?**

BC: You are referring to clothing, obviously, which is the fun part of Planepack, I think. A long time ago I discovered that it's essential to wear the right colours that suit you. As I am a professional stylist I am able to advise potential clients on the best clothes that suit them determined by their hair, eye and skin colour.

JR: What's a stylist?

BG: The stylist is a person who is qualified to work with you as an individual or with an organisation to assist them to dress and pack and look the best that they can. So my advice is generally to assist women to travel lightly, wearing the clothes that might suit them. So that is generally driven by the colouring.

JR: In terms of colouring, are there different colours that one person should wear and colours that they shouldn't wear?

BG: Oh yes, most definitely, and as I said it's determined by your colouring, by your hair and your eye and your skin colouring. So my base colour for example when I travel is black or grey. My wardrobe is essentially shades of black or grey, but I add a little bit of colour for that evening zing. So if I am, you know, having a drink on a terrazza or somewhere, it's lovely to be able to wear a brighter colour, something other than during-the-day-wear but keeping to those principles of travel light. So I have a very strict wardrobe that I like to travel with.

𝒥ℛ: **What do you travel with?**

𝐵𝒢: Good question, there is a list actually. There are many sites online that offer packing lists and my packing list is available on my blog, which is called planepack.com.au. I travel exceedingly lightly and this is a methodology that I have honed over the last few years. My list contains things like: one skirt, one pair of trousers, one pair of shorts, five pairs of underpants, two bras, two pairs of socks, one pair of tights, one jacket, and three little T-shirts that might be in colour, and then I have a pair of sandals and I have a pair of very good comfortable shoes that I fly in, I walk in and I wear just about every single day. And of course I take along some cosmetics.

𝒥ℛ: **And a handbag?**

𝐵𝒢: Yes, I do take a handbag with me and I travel with a handbag that I have used I think for quite a few years. It's a very comfortable soft leather handbag. It can be squished easily under the seat in front me when I fly and I travel with only the essentials with me that I may need to use on the plane, but then that bag obviously becomes my travel bag or my handbag when I am travelling around Europe or Asia, or where it might be I can take it to the beach if I want to. It has multiple uses.

JR: Does a raincoat or umbrella or poncho figure in your list?

BC: Well, I wouldn't travel with an umbrella, because an umbrella is something that might be confiscated at customs because of the pointy end. I actually have a snub-nosed umbrella but I am reluctant to test that because I would hate to lose it. I think that's a good question about the poncho or raincoat. I travel with what's called a splash jacket. It's a very nice one that I bought a few years ago in New Zealand and it has sleeves that I can unzip and a hood that I can unzip. So it's multipurpose and it's a nice colour—it certainly kind of livens up the wardrobe. I can wear it as a coat or just as a waistcoat, and I usually wear that on the plane.

JR: Could also double as a dressing gown I imagine?

BC: Oh no, no, I do carry a dressing gown, I forgot to mention that is part of my
 Planepack list. I have a night dress—a nightie—and I have a very light dressing gown which again I found quite a few years ago and it's leopard print. So I suppose that could double up as a top too if I want to wear it as a wrap.

JR: You mentioned two pairs of shoes, one you will be wearing, the other would be in your hand luggage. Do you carry thongs?

BG: I do actually carry thongs, and I am quite comfortable with leaving them behind as well if I need to because people have asked me, they say what happens if you want to buy stuff overseas? I am not that strict that I say you can't buy and, yes indeed, if you want to buy something and fit it into your suitcase or into your carry-on then toss out the thongs or something else that you are quite happy to get rid of.

JR: And sport attires: a pair of swimming togs or costume?

BG: Yes I do travel with a costume and I have a very nice light sarong which is actually a synthetic material so it dries very quickly. So I can easily wear that from the beach to the shops. I just tie it around my waist or tie it as a little dress.

JR: Some people like to go jogging when they have arrived in the country of their destination. What footwear would somebody who jogs be able to wear?

BG: That's an interesting question and I think that the comfortable shoes would most probably be the joggers as well, although I personally am not a jogger. My husband who travels with me is and he would include a pair of jogging shoes as part of his wardrobe.

JR: **In terms of pashminas or silk shawl or something similar, would you pack that in your handbag or in your carry-on?**

BG: I would usually pack that in my handbag so that I can it use on the plane, because the planes are quite chilly and the blanket is often not enough.

JR: **Where have you travelled with your Planepack and tested it?**

BG: I have travelled to New Zealand, I have travelled to Vietnam, I have been to Serbia and Montenegro and to South Africa and to the United States. So it's quite a few destinations. I have only tested it in warmer climates; I have yet to test in cold climates. I have full confidence that those Planepack tips will work. What I would do is exchange the short-sleeved tops for nice long-sleeved fine merino tops and I would layer other clothes.

JR: **In terms of textiles for the clothing that you take, do you have a preference for wools or cotton?**

BG: That's an excellent question. Personally I have a preference for natural fibres. A few years ago I thought I would travel with some synthetic fibres, a lovely pair of slacks and a top because they can roll up so easily, but what I found is that they are very heavy. So my preference is still for cotton, silk, light wool, cashmere, and those, while they might be a little bit bulkier, they are simply lighter.

JR: In terms of looking after them, the maintenance and care of your items when travelling, what principles for cleanliness do you follow?

BC: Yes, well it depends on where you stay. If I holiday in places where I stay in hotels, usually the hotels offer you a laundry service. So what I would do is once a week I would bundle everything up, put it in a bag, they would wash it and return it, washed and ironed and the prices are not exorbitant. If you are not able to do that I would suggest you buy some kind of washing powder overseas and wash your clothes using that. I don't think you should travel with washing powder or any liquids.

JR: In terms of in-hotel laundry, do you have any suggestions to make sure that your clothes come back to you?

BC: Well, that's an interesting point, I have never had an issue, but on that point I don't travel with things that are too precious to me. I travel with very practical clothes and I find that I travel with very similar clothes over the years, so my aim in travelling is not to dress in my most sumptuous clothes that I might own, but to be very practical and then to add a touch of glamour with an accessory.

JR: **In terms of versatility of your clothing, you mentioned being able to be flexible with your clothes. What would you recommend going from day wear to evening wear?**

BC: That's a good question. To address your question about flexibility, I make sure that everything works with everything else in terms of colour, that's important. So it's very easy to match a top with shorts, top with skirt, top with trousers. To go from day wear to evening wear I would most probably wear a pair of trousers or the skirt perhaps with one of the coloured tops and I would throw on a very nice necklace and, as you say, the pashmina if I am travelling, or a lovely silk scarf.

JR: **Footwear, what would you wear?**

BC: Footwear, yes, my sandals that I take along are usually [fine] and if I wear long trousers, then I would wear the same footwear that I travel in. I can assure you nobody ever notices your footwear when you are travelling.

JR: **What about protection of valuable items: your wallet, your passport, your keys? How do you protect those?**

BC: I also slip in a very small over-the-shoulder bag that I can wear on my body if I need to. I generally don't travel with keys, I leave that to my husband or otherwise I take one key if I need to get back into my house. My passport is usually locked away either in the room or in the passport safe in the hotel and I don't take any other things of great value other than my phone and I don't travel with much cash; I pay for everything with the card. So if I do have to carry my passport, my phone and my wallet with me it's usually on that bag which I can wear over my shoulder and if I really feel uncomfortable about it I could wear it under my jacket.

JR: In terms of identification of your luggage and your items, do you have any tips on how to make sure that everything comes back to you if lost?

BC: Well, if I am travelling with it in my hands it doesn't get lost and getting lost is a very good question, because that's one of the issues that drove me to travel with hand luggage and carry-on early, because in recent years my suitcase has been lost twice, once for three days and once for six weeks, and that is what actually decided me to travel with hand luggage only. So my luggage is really never out of my hands.

JR: When we go through airport checking and the security wand goes past us, is there anything that you are wearing that would draw attention to you?

BC: No because I usually travel with soft shoes and I don't travel with chunky jewellery. I do take some jewellery with me. I don't travel with a belt. The biggest benefit of travelling light with carry-on luggage is that you don't have to wait for a suitcase at the carousel and that can save you half an hour to three-quarters of an hour when you exit. And for me personally the best experience is walking out of the plane, walking through passport control, leaving the baggage claim carousel to my left or right and walking straight through the exit.

JR: **Heading for the taxi.**

BC: Absolutely right.

JR: **How well received has Planepack been by your colleagues?**

BC: Very well; they are intrigued by it. The plan is, as I mentioned, I have a blog at the moment that I am writing and I am slowly building up a following. When I have mentioned it to my friends they all said, 'We will buy the book, we'd love to have the book,' so hopefully this will become a book. I would like to write more about product, maybe do some product reviews. I would say generally it's well received and people surprise me by saying, 'Goodness, this is the way that I have been travelling for a while!' and I hope to interview those people. Some of my friends of course say, 'Well, I never will be able to do that!' and it is my mission in life to try and assist them through that process.

JR: What is it they perceive prevents them from travelling light?

BC: I think they need to have more clothes with them and my argument is to persuade them that they can actually travel comfortably, they can look as good as they want to and they don't need to burden themselves with the handicap of a large heavy suitcase. Just because you can take it on the airplane doesn't mean that you have to.

JR: When we are travelling and we find all sorts of trinkets or clothing or books that we would like to bring home with us, how does Planepack manage that?

BC: I would suggest that you post them back. That would be my first suggestion. Alternatively, if you are happy to travel back with luggage in the hold—and it's usually easier on the way back home—you could just buy a small inexpensive suitcase and put those things into it. Generally there is room for an extra little trinket or two in the Planepack handluggage and the thing to remember is always to check with airlines because some airlines have different rules. I am flying with another airline domestically soon and I see that they allow up to

12 kilograms, so in fact with some airlines you can buy capacity for more handheld luggage.

JR: What extra items would you take with you?

BC: If I were to fly? I hadn't thought about that, I am so strict with myself on limiting the amount of things that I carry. Actually I think the thing that I would like to find a better way of travelling with is a hat, because I like to wear a fedora in the summer and they don't squash up very nicely. When I was travelling through an airport about a year or so ago I saw a woman carrying a beautiful hat bag; it was a rigid hat bag and I thought, 'Oh, that would be nice,' but I am really not sure that I want to add another bag to what I have in my hands. So I think maybe I am looking for hats that look elegant but fold up nicely.

JR: Will they be wool hats?

BC: No, I am thinking about summer hats for the extreme heat. I did buy myself a nice one recently that's got a mosquito net for countries or areas where you might be plagued by flies or mosquitoes, so I might try that one out next time.

JR: When you are packing your clothes—your items in your luggage—do you have a system of packing where one goes in before the next?

BG: Yes, certainly it's always good. I always pack my sandals first, I pack the rigid things at the bottom and then I roll and pack my soft clothes around the shoes and around the harder items. I use the roll-up model, but then as I get to the top of the suitcase they become flatter. So it's a combination. There are definitely people online who show videos on how you can pack beautifully. My principle is just take the right things with you and make sure that it's not heavy enough. What I generally do is I weigh my bag before my cosmetics, because the cosmetics are very heavy. Cosmetics are something that you can play around with as well and to decide on what you want to take with you when you are going.

JR: **Towards the end of your travels you might have a few items that are soiled and need the wash. How does Planepack manage those items?**

BG: I usually have a small laundry bag that I put in, and my suitcase has a partition that's kept away from the others, so I would put the soiled clothes into those.

JR: **With your cosmetics do you travel with the 100ml containers? How do you manage all the fluids?**

BG: Yes absolutely, that is something you have to be very strict and manage carefully because if you travel with anything over 100ml in your hand luggage it will get confiscated at customs. I buy those clear plastic containers and I decant some of my cosmetics into those or otherwise before I travel I make sure that I have my essential items, like toothpaste, for example, in 100ml containers. I also build up a collection of samples that I get during the year—you know what it's like, you can go into a shop and they say try our products—and then I use those when I am overseas, so that's always fun because it gives me an opportunity to do something different.

JR: In terms of taking care of your luggage itself what principles do you apply?

BG: Are you talking about the bag itself? Well, I have been using the same bag now for 10 or more years and I like a rigid bag. I find those hard-case bags are very useful and remember, if I am carrying it, it doesn't get thrown around as much as it would if I was putting it in the hold. I think the softer bags are nice because they are lighter. I am not really concerned that they might get torn or ripped because they are always within my reach, but the other reason why I like a rigid bag is if you have a long layover at an airport you can use it as a footrest. So it doubles up as something en route.

JR: So if you are staying over and there have been some timing issues with the flights you can use the luggage as a footrest.

BG: Exactly, that's right.

JR: **When you are in the plane, in your seat, where do you place your carry-on luggage?**

BG: In the carry-on luggage holds above me. A friend of mine has mentioned that she might have an issue raising seven kilograms above her head and my advice in that case would be to ask for help from the airline staff to do that, because you are within your rights to carry that weight on board with you.

JR: **When you talk about Planepack as a venture for Bobby Graham how did you come to this name?**

BG: That's an interesting question. It arose last year: I studied further, I studied to become a stylist and as part of that course I had to put forward some kind of a business proposal about where I would like to go forward in my styling career. Because my friends had mentioned that they love to know more about travelling light, packing, etc, the name came to me and I had to seek something that I could research as a domain name for a website. And because it's all about packing and it's all about travelling light and it's about planes, the name Planepack just came to me and it stuck and I quite like it; and it was available so people have responded positively and said, 'Oh you can do other things as well. You can do travel pack or you can do camping pack or you can do baby pack or you can do . . .', I don't know what else, it sort of resonates with people. I thought it was quite a nice name.

JR: How does the world find out about Planepack?

BG: At the moment the world can find out about Planepack by following me on my blog—planepack.com.au—where I am writing about the how and the why of Planepack itself. I hope it's an entertaining blog where readers can read about the experiences that I have had travelling, because since that long ago trip when I travelled with 14 additional T-shirts I have travelled quite a bit more and I have also done a bit of sailing and I have holidayed in a mobile home, and all those experiences have led me to believe strongly in something like Planepack. So that's a good way of finding out more about Planepack and of course through my social media: I have a Planepack Facebook, I have Planepack Instagram, I have Planepack on Pinterest. So there are quite a few ways that people can find Planepack.

JR: Thank you, Bobby Graham. This has been a recording with Bobby Graham of BG Publishers about Planepack travel light experience. © Voiceprint/Fiona Rothchilds™ 2017. Thank you.

www.ingramcontent.com/pod-product-compliance
Lightning Source LLC
Chambersburg PA
CBHW062035290426
44109CB00026B/2639